7 Most Powerful Prayers
(from the Kingdom of Judah)

Fearlessness, Hope, and Miracles for Your Everyday Circumstances

W. D. CROWDER

ISBN: 172345625X
ISBN-13: 978-1723456251

DEDICATION

This book is lovingly and gratefully dedicated to my dear brother Michael who has become such an inspiration to me over the last few years. You have prevailed through and overcome truly impossible and undeserved circumstances without complaining all the while. That is real Godliness in action. Thank you for being an example (to me and to us all) of real-life encouragement, fearlessness, hope, and miracles in your everyday circumstances, dear brother.

CONTENTS

Map of the Kingdoms of Judah and Israel

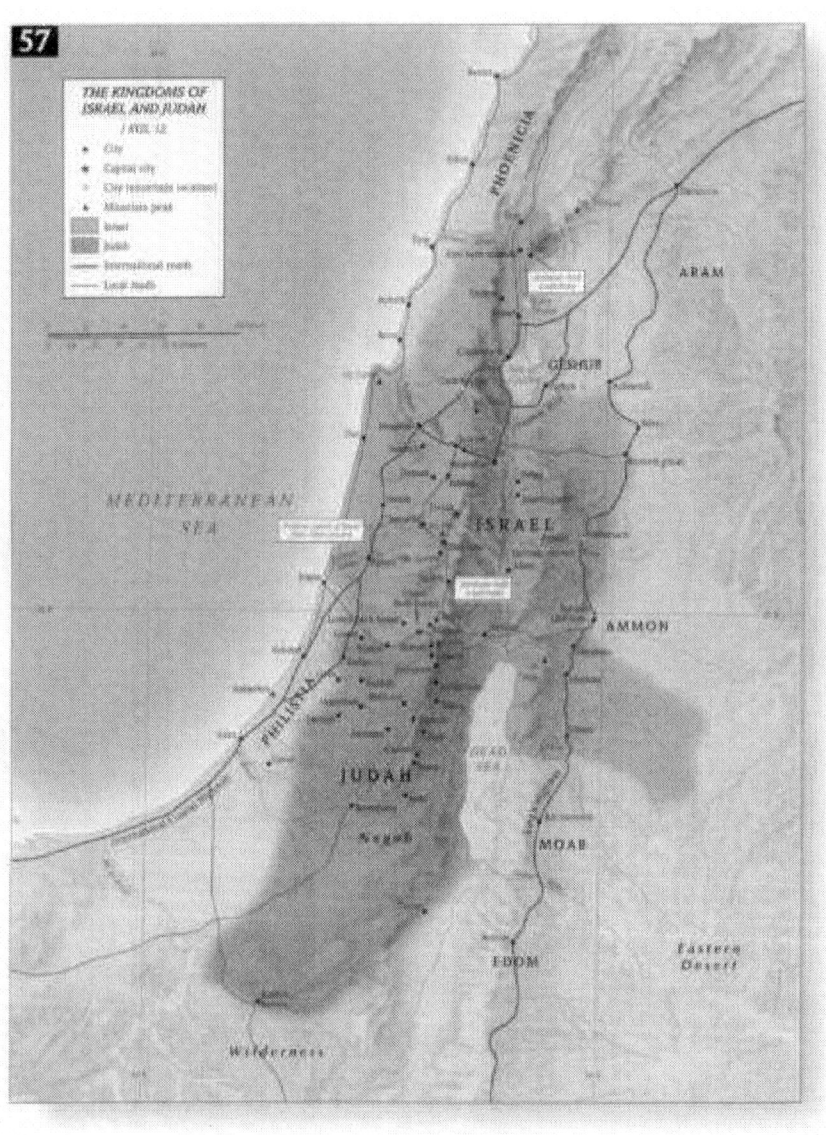

ACKNOWLEDGMENTS

I want to extend a special thanks to the following people who materially contributed to the start of this book in some form or fashion:

Ian of Bible Baptist Church in Malta, whose own life struggles and triumphs over them, along with our emails back and forth (once we had left the Christian country and original "lands of the Bible" island of Malta) inspired me to start writing again with *The Three Miraculous Prayers of King Hezekiah* five years ago.

Pastor Francesco of the Potters' House here in Malta, whose sermons, encouragement, and supporting prayers have helped to keep me on track through researching and writing this book and especially in the months, weeks, and days leading up to starting it.

My encouraging friends of the Potter's House in Malta, who have helped encourage me to keep up the good work and "continue the race" even through fierce opposition and ongoing health struggles over the years. Justin, Leon, Anthony, Terry, Kimberly, and Christina especially have helped to keep me going.

Pastor Rick of the Potter's House in South Carolina, who was responsible for giving me my second start in speaking to churches (several years ago, after a hiatus of 15 years) especially in Europe and Great Britain.

Keith, my dear friend (in "the Potteries") and publicist from Stoke on Trent in Great Britain. He has always been my biggest fan and most ardent supporter of my writing, since the days of *We Three Kings: Two Journeys of the Magi* back in 2001. We have come far together, Keith! Thank you for all the years of encouragement to continue writing, publishing, and promoting these books!

Valerie and Claire my dear friends who used to live in Malta and are now back in England, who have gone above and beyond the call of duty and the extra mile in their heartfelt friendship and support of me and my family in these encouraging books and church speaking trips.

My brothers Michael and Jared who have always been there for me and served as sounding boards for the book ideas and first drafts of them for the last several books in the "Divine Encounters of the Bible Series."

My parents who have always encouraged me in my writing endeavors all of my life. We sure miss you dad (but are glad you have gone home to heaven). We will see you again one day. Thank you both for the support over the years!

My dear children and wife Anna who give me that extra reason to get out of bed each and every day. You help to provide the joy in my life that makes it all worthwhile.

Thank you from my heart to all of you. I could not have even begun this latest monumental project without each person!

Also by W.D. Crowder

"The Divine Encounters Bible Series"

We Three Kings: Two Journeys of the Magi

The Three Miraculous Prayers of King Hezekiah: A Good Man's
Example for Our Own Troubled Times

Lives of the Great Apostles: The Real Life Rest of the Story of the
Men Who Walked Beside Jesus

God Will Never Abandon You! Biblical and Personal Examples of
God's Everlasting Faithfulness

Reigns of The Kings of Judah (8 "Good" Kings)

Rehoboam (933-916) seventeen years

Abijam (915-913) three years

Asa (Good) (912-872) forty-one years

Jehoshaphat (Good) (874-850) twenty-five years

Jehoram (850-843) eight years

Ahaziah (843) one year

Athaliah (843-837) six years

Joash (Good) (843-803) forty years

Amaziah (Good) (803-775) 29 years

Azariah (Uzziah) (Good) (787-735) fifty-two years

Jotham (Good) (749-734) sixteen years

Ahaz (741-726) sixteen years

Hezekiah (Good) (726-697) 29 years

Manasseh (Became Good) (697-642) fifty-five years

Amon (641-640) two years

Josiah (Good) (639-608) thirty-one years

Jehoahaz (608) three months

Jehoiachim (608-597) eleven years

Jehoiachin (597) three months

Zedekiah (597-586) eleven years

1 WHAT HAS GONE WRONG WITH THE WORLD WE LIVE IN TODAY?

We live in a world twisted by sin and sorrow thousands of years ago. If you are like most people today, this means that you suffer. Wars, sickness, famine, earthquakes, tsunamis, typhoons, hurricanes, school shootings, mass murders, wildfires, landslides, terrorism, and so much more rock our groaning planet on a constant, even daily basis.

On a more personal level, you experience pain, personal loss, feelings of inadequacy, lack of direction and purpose, drug addiction or opioid dependence, abandonment and divorce, addiction to alcohol, loneliness, despair, depression, darkness, sickness, financial hardship, and perhaps most debilitating of all--- FEAR.

You fear the unknown, the uncertainty of a future that appears to be getting worse (and not better) for you personally and the world in general. Politicians and world leaders, technological advances and progress, and even social media all promised you a future that would be brighter and better than your all-too-present reality. Looking at your own life in particular and around the world everywhere today, this certainly does not appear to be the case.

Where are the answers to all of these very real, personal, painful, and legitimate problems you see and feel all around you? Where is the hope; where are the solutions? You may even find yourself honestly questioning is God still out there? Is He listening? Does He care at all? Why does it seem like my earnest cries for help and my prayers sometimes fall on proverbial "deaf ears"? Has God entirely abandoned our world to sin, suffering, sorrow, death, and sadness and just moved on to someplace else?

Considering the sad state of our world today, no one could blame you for asking such direct, honest, and intensely personal and relevant questions. God does not blame you for asking these kinds of totally honest questions. He is not angry with you. He loves us all so desperately, even when it does not feel like it or appear that way from your own personal pain and suffering and looking at the world you see all around you now.

In the story that follows we are about to embark on a time-travelling experience and journey back to a world and time that was very much like the days we live in now. We are going to look back at a period in the shared story of this earth when there was the same darkness and despair, hardship, fear, loss, death, grief, and doubt.

The bad news is that we've been here before friends. The great news is that God Himself reached out to that day and age in a mighty and powerful way that made people's ears tingle when they heard about it. He heard the cries of people suffering much like us in their own daily pain, sorrow, and grief.

He performed enormous miraculous answers to prayer that were so powerful then that people recorded them thousands of years ago, and we are still talking about them today. He provided powerful help and supernatural relief with forgiveness of major personal mistakes, deliverance from hopelessness and bondage, wisdom in dark and dangerous times, healing of crippling sickness that should lead to death, and even financial assistance.

Strap yourselves in and close your eyes a moment for a time

travelling odyssey like no other. Now open them up again…

You have just arrived in the year 1,200 B.C. You have traveled back in time over 3,000 years. Welcome to a troubled world surprisingly like ours today. Welcome to the Kingdom of Judah.

2 THE JOURNEY BEGINS

What's So Special About Ancient Israel?

Climbing out of the time machine and observing ancient Israel, you notice a few interesting characteristics. The Israelites were faithful enough in following God's appointed leaders Moses and Joshua that God helped them to overcome their enemies and to settle the land. The problems of the Israelites began soon after as the next generations quickly forgot about the deeds of their great and mighty God and what he had done for their parents, grandparents, and other ancestors.

In only a handful of generations, the Israelites had picked up the bad habits of worshipping false gods created by the local people they did not drive out (as God commanded them). This quickly led ancient Israel into a vicious downward spiral. God would no longer assist them when they did not seek out His help any longer. The once-powerful Israelites were soon overrun by their enemies and living in continuous defeat and fear.

What followed for the next several hundred years was a cyclic period of the Judges. As you watch these Judges doing their part to rally the Israelites to serve God and overthrow their enemies all around, you quickly come to the conclusion that the Judges were more like warrior leaders who also had the function of settling disputes between peoples of the land in the period of peace that followed their deliverance. God raised these men (and one woman) up to become more than conquerors with His help.

Following along with the account written in the book of Judges in the Old Testament of the Bible, you can see it unfold before your very eyes. At one point in time, a group of Middle Eastern people known as the Midianites overran ancient Israel. Things quickly went from bad to worse.

> "The Israelites did evil in the eyes of the Lord, and for seven years he gave them into the hands of the Midianites. Because the power of Midian was so oppressive, the Israelites prepared shelters for themselves in mountain clefts, caves, and strongholds.
>
> Whenever the Israelites planted their crops, the Midianites, Amalekites, and other eastern peoples invaded the country. They camped on the land and ruined the crops all the way to Gaza and did not spare a living thing for Israel, neither sheep nor cattle nor donkeys.
>
> They came up with their livestock and their tents like swarms of locusts. It was impossible to count them or their camels; they invaded the land to ravage it. Midian so impoverished the Israelites that they cried out to the Lord for help." (Judges 6:1-6).

You can already picture how bad this must have been from the way that the Israelites were putting together safe houses wherever they could to protect their very lives from the enemy. Yet it was a losing battle. The Midianites simply stole all of the food the Israelites produced each season. This kept them in a constant state of fear and bondage. Finally the oppression of the enemy had grown so great that the Israelites turned to God again for His help.

As you picture this whole sad scenario unfolding before your eyes, it might strike you that there are parallels in your own life with this story today. So many people allow riches, possessions, and distractions to take their eyes off of God. Individuals who have grown too comfortable no longer have the same need for God and His help in their lives.

Before we cast the proverbial first stone at what we see happening in this picture of Ancient Israel, it is important to remember that nearly all of us are guilty of doing this very same thing at some point in our own lives. We may not have false gods made from stone or gold and silver, yet we do have our glossier, modern day versions in the worship of money, beauty, celebrities, pleasures, fancy cars, big houses, computers, the Internet, social media, and especially Facebook.

Yet when the people of Ancient Israel had enough of their miserable and intolerable circumstances, they remembered the very God that they had abandoned and turned back to Him. At this point, God found His unlikely hero whom He would use to restore the lost independence and prosperity to Israel. Enter onto the scene the hero of this our first time travelling adventure story--- Gideon.

Gideon was not the superhero you might expect that God would select to work with and through the trying circumstances of the Israelites. He was no strongman Sampson or wisest King Solomon. Yet somehow he was just the man the God of the universe sought.

> "The angel of the Lord came and sat down under the oak in Ophrah that belonged to Joash the Abiezrite, where his son Gideon was threshing wheat in a winepress to keep it from the Midianites. When the angel of the Lord appeared to Gideon, he said, 'The Lord is with you, mighty warrior'." (Judges 6:11-12).

By the angel's words we can see the irony here. Gideon was hiding in a hollowed out area or cave so that he could safely and securely thresh out his wheat. You can't blame him from wanting to keep it from the scary enemy hordes who seemed more like an army of locusts than men.

Yet clearly this was not a literal "mighty warrior" in the flesh. Either the angel of the Lord was displaying a sense of humor, or he wanted to build up Gideon to be the man that he might become with time and the right divine encouragement. Gideon's reply spoke volumes about where he was at personally in those early days.

> "Pardon me, my lord," Gideon replied, "but if the Lord is with us, why has all this happened to us? Where are all His wonders that our ancestors told us about when they said, 'Did not the Lord bring us up out of Egypt?' But now the Lord has abandoned us and given us into the hand of Midian. The Lord turned to him and said, 'Go in the strength you have and save Israel out of Midian's hand. Am I not sending you'?" (Judges 6:13-14).

These were honest and real but challenging questions, respectfully addressed to God. The Lord showed great patience with Gideon during this first verbal exchange. His answer to the issue of "why us," was that *I* have chosen *you* to be the instrument of *my* deliverance. This only begged still more questions from Gideon, who seems more than unsure of himself in the early parts of this intriguing true story.

> "Pardon me, my lord," Gideon replied, 'but how can I save Israel? My clan is the weakest in Manasseh, and I am the least in my family'." (Judges 6:15).

Now we come to the real heart of the matter in this story. Gideon this man of ancient Israel was simply afraid. Like so many of us in our own lives today, his fear held sway over his entire life. When God reassured Gideon that he was the man for the big task, he immediately began making what were legitimate and true excuses.

The way Gideon saw himself here speaks volumes as to the condition of his oppressed and bound life. We have all been there standing in his shoes at one point or another in our own stories.

> "The Lord answered, 'I will be with you, and you will strike down all the Midianites, leaving none alive'. Gideon replied, 'If I now have found favor in your eyes, give me a sign that it is really you talking to me. Please do not go away until I come back and bring my offering and set it before you'. And the Lord said, 'I will wait until you return'." (Judges 6:16-18).

This was only the first of many tests that Gideon would put God through in order to prove that He was faithful enough to overcome Gideon's deep-seated personal fears.

> "The angel of God said to him, 'Take the meat and the unleavened bread, place them on this rock, and pour out the broth.' And Gideon did so. Then the angel of the Lord touched the meat and the unleavened bread with the tip of the staff that was in his hand. Fire flared from the rock, consuming the meat and the bread. And the angel of the Lord disappeared." (Judges 6:20-21).

This was enough to help Gideon over his initial fears of taking on the job as deliverer and mighty warrior who could be used by God to save Israel from her enemies. When next we catch up with him, Gideon has found sufficient courage to tackle the oppressors in an initial action.

> "Now all the Midianites, Amalekites, and other eastern peoples joined forces and crossed over the Jordan and camped in the Valley of Jezreel. Then the Spirit of the Lord came on Gideon, and he blew a trumpet, summoning the Abiezrites to follow him. He sent messengers throughout Manasseh, calling them to arms, and also into Asher, Zebulun, and Naphtali, so that they too went up to meet

them." (Judges 6:33-35).

What happened to Gideon the cowardly? He has experienced a divine encounter with the almighty God of the universe in the interim. The Spirit of God fell on him and the otherwise fearful man suddenly became Gideon the courageous. Like a true "mighty warrior" he set about gathering an army from all of the surrounding parts of Ancient Israel. You might think at this point in the story that Gideon has received all of the supernatural power that he needs to see the battle against the enemy hordes through to victory. Not so fast.

> "Gideon said to God, 'If you will save Israel by my hand as you have promised – look, I will place a wool fleece on the threshing floor. If there is dew only on the fleece and all the ground is dry, then I will know that you will save Israel by my hand, as you said.' And that is what happened. Gideon rose early the next day; he squeezed the fleece and wrung out the dew—a bowlful of water." (Judges 6:36-38).

Wait a second, what just happened to our hero, God's "mighty warrior?" It looks like Gideon assembled his army together and then suddenly took his eyes off of God. Gideon the powerful was suddenly Gideon the wavering again.

It was as if Gideon had gone from his army camp and returned back to the cave where he had been hiding and threshing wheat at the beginning of the story all over again. Yet God in His goodness honored sincere and heartfelt questions coming from a willing heart but a mind still paralyzed by fear and indecision. So God honored Gideon's latest challenge and proved Himself to the once-again trembling hero.

> "Then Gideon said to God, 'Do not be angry with me. Let me make just one more request. Allow me one more test with the fleece, but this time make the fleece dry and let the

ground be covered with dew. That night God did so. Only the fleece was dry; all the ground was covered with dew." (Judges 6:39-40).

With your unique advantage of being an omniscient time-travelling observer of this story, it is easy to make fun of and scoff at Gideon's sheer nerve. The man has now requested his third test of the God of the universe, who has already worked two prior amazing miracles for him personally to build up his courage, strengthen his faith, and stretch his belief in the supernatural. Surely God would have seen enough of Gideon "the weak" by this point and would simply find someone else to get the job done.

The good news for all of us today (as it was for Gideon then) is though none of us are perfect, God works with imperfect people. We are all that He has to work with here on earth after all.

Yet stop for a minute and ask yourself a hard, soul-searching question: Have you ever been afraid of your own personal demons in life? These could be any number of subtle or overt attacks that assail and paralyze you. The Bible teaches that the enemy of your soul (the devil) prowls around like a roaring lion, seeking those whom he may devour. (I Peter 5:8).

Today you might be wracked by fear, despair, and hopelessness: afraid that you are not good enough, fearful that you will fail like everyone else in your family before you already has for generations. You could live in fear of losing your job, your youth, your "good looks," your spouse, your children, your health, your house, your possessions, your life, and even your mind. When we put this story into modern day terms, suddenly you may get quiet and find yourself not laughing at Gideon's expense anymore. The simple truth is that if we are lucky, we are Gideon at both his worst *and* his best.

Gideon At Last Rises Up To Take on the Midianites

With Gideon's third test of God out of the way, he was ready to take on the enemy.

> "Early in the morning, Gideon and all his men camped at the spring of Harod. The camp of Midian was north of them in the valley near the hills of Moreh. The Lord said to Gideon, 'You have too many men. I cannot deliver Midian into their hands, or Israel would boast against me, 'My own strength has saved me.' Now announce to the army, 'Anyone who trembles with fear may turn back and leave Mount Gilead'.' So twenty-two thousand men left, while ten thousand remained."

> "But the Lord said to Gideon, 'There are still too many men. Take them down to the water, and I will thin them out for you there. If I say, 'This one shall go with you,' he shall go; but if I say, 'This one shall not go with you,' he shall not go."

> "So Gideon took the men down to the water. There the Lord told him, 'Separate those who lap the water with their tongues as a dog laps from those who kneel down to drink.' Three hundred of them drank from cupped hands, lapping like dogs. All the rest got down on their knees to drink."

> "The Lord said to Gideon, 'With the three hundred men that lapped I will save you and give the Midianites into your hands. Let all the others go home.' So Gideon sent the rest of the Israelites home but kept the three hundred, who took over the provisions and trumpets of the others.

> "Now the camp of Midian lay below him in the valley. During that night the Lord said to Gideon, 'Get up, go down against the camp, because I am going to give it into your

hands. If you are afraid to attack, go down to the camp with your servant Purah and listen to what they are saying. Afterward, you will be encouraged to attack the camp.'

So he and Purah his servant went down to the outposts of the camp. "The Midianites, the Amalekites, and all the other eastern peoples had settled in the valley, thick as locusts. Their camels could no more be counted than the sand on the seashore." (Judges 7:1-12).

You may not be surprised by this point that God tested Gideon's newfound superman faith again by whittling down the hero's army from 32,000 to a mere 300. This was a severe blow to Gideon's confidence as he looked out on an enemy army and camp so vast that he could not begin to count them. Gideon had grown enough in his faith to not ask God for another miraculous sign. But you can see him standing there looking down on the enormous enemy army, and you know that he wants one desperately badly.

So God intervened and showed poor Gideon the wavering that He would work the necessary miracles to overthrow the enemy of the Israelites. He offered Gideon another powerful proof that God was truly in what was now starting to look like a hopeless quest.

"Gideon arrived just as a man was telling a friend his dream. 'I had a dream," he was saying. 'A round loaf of barley bread came tumbling into the Midianite camp. It struck the tent with such force that the tent overturned and collapsed.'

His friend responded, 'This can be nothing other than the sword of Gideon son of Joash, the Israelite. God has given the Midianites and the whole camp into his hands'."

"When Gideon heard the dream and its interpretation, he bowed down and worshipped [God]. He returned to the camp of Israel and called out, 'Get up! The Lord has given the Midianite camp into your hands.' (Judges 7:13-15).

We don't know whether it was God or Gideon who originated the plan that the tiny Israelite army put into place for the late night ambush battle. Certainly the time which you are witnessing had yet to see a military manual written to help out would-be aspiring military commanders like our hero Gideon. Yet whoever's idea it was, the plan was bold, clever, and deadly effective.

> "Dividing the three hundred men into three companies, he placed trumpets and empty jars in the hands of all of them, with torches inside. 'Watch me,' he told them. 'Follow my lead. When I get to the edge of the camp, do exactly as I do. When I and all who are with me blow our trumpets, then from all around the camp blow yours and shout, 'For the Lord and for Gideon'."

> "Gideon and the hundred men with him reached the edge of the camp at the beginning of the middle watch, just after they had changed the guard. They blew their trumpets and broke the jars that were in their hands. The three companies blew the trumpets and smashed the jars.

> Grasping the torches in their left hands and holding in their right hands the trumpets they were to blow, they shouted, 'A sword for the Lord and for Gideon!' While each man held his position around the camp, all the Midianites ran, crying out as they fled."

> "When the three hundred trumpets sounded, the Lord caused the men throughout the camp to turn on each other with their swords. The army fled...and they pursued the Midianites. Gideon sent messengers throughout the hill country of Ephraim, saying, 'Come down against the Midianites and seize the waters of the Jordan ahead of them...

So all the men of Ephraim were called out and they seized the waters of the Jordan…They also captured two of the Midianite leaders, Raven and Wolf. They killed Raven at the rock of Raven and Wolf at the winepress of Wolf. They pursued the Midianites and brought the heads of Raven and Wolf to Gideon, who was by the Jordan." (Judges 7:16-25).

Personal Application for Your Life Today

You have watched Gideon transform from the fearful, shaken, hiding (in the cave from his enemies) coward to the fearless warrior-judge. The same God who saved and supernaturally empowered Gideon to rise up above his fear to tackle the enemies of his time is still helping individuals do this today. My own life is a classic example of the story of Gideon in action.

I have realized that my personal testimony is much like Gideon's in many ways. I can be like Gideon both at his best and at his worst. This is to say that when I am Gideon the "weaker," I am fearful and sometimes downright overwhelmed and even discouraged by the numerous challenges I face in my own life. These have included both severe battles with my health personally and significant financial difficulties. At times they have seemed like a veritable army of locusts seeking to steal, kill, devour, and destroy everything good in my life.

Like a number of individuals living today, I have stood at the edge of the precipice of intense difficulties in life and stared down into the abyss of potential failure. I can tell you from personal experience that it was black. If you are like many people in the troubled world in which we live today, then you probably have been to this dark place (a "valley of the shadow of death," the Bible calls it) before yourself. It is not a point to which you would want to return if you could possibly avoid it.

On the other hand, I can also be (and aspire to continuously be) Gideon "the stronger." When you and I do things fully in God's power and strength, and not just trusting in and relying on our own efforts that we hope He will decide to bless (out of His abundant mercy), then we attain the levels that Gideon experienced personally in defeating his numerous enemies. In my own life, these have been those happiest of times when I was writing, speaking at churches and on radio stations, and meeting and encouraging people at bookstore signings and church groups.

When you find yourself at these crossroads of trouble and testing in your life (and they do and will come for certain, of that you can be sure), then you need to remember three things.

1. God overcame Gideon's extreme fear of losing what he had and raised him up to deliver his people from their enemies and brutal oppression.

2. God also overcame my own fears in my desperate needs, personal circumstances and unknown wasting illness (about which I go into great detail and painful details in my prior book all about hope and miracles, _God Will Never Abandon You!_) to raise me up to write these encouraging books and to speak in front of churches, pastors, individuals, and on radio stations in America and Europe (and I can freely admit to you that I am _not_ a naturally gifted speaker).

3. God will overcome your own personal fears too and raise you up to be more than a conqueror today (like Gideon the stronger) if you only will ask Him to do it and then trust Him.

While you are pondering the truth that there is a little bit of Gideon in all of us, we are firing up the time travelling odyssey again. In our next stop, we will arrive at our ultimate destination--- the most powerfully praying Kingdom of Judah.

3 THE PRAYERS FOR FINANCIAL SALVATION FROM KING DAVID

King David Was The Original "Man After God's Own Heart"

As we survey the scene unfolding before us, you learn something you might never have realized about the Kingdom of Judah. It was actually founded by one of the most famous characters from the Bible--- King David. You can see him standing there as a heroic young man, full of life, vitality, and promise.

From a young and early age, David had learned personally what it meant to seek out and trust God. He testified in his youth (to the King of Israel before him Saul) that when he was tending his father Jesse's sheep, God helped him to overcome a lion and a bear that attacked. King Saul could only be impressed by this claim.

He allowed the youth David to fight the enemy of the Israelites--- Goliath the giant. No one else in the entire country had the courage to do personal combat with this monster of a man who came to challenge the armies of Israel each and every day for more than a month. King David without any armor or even a sword battled Goliath with only a sling shot and a few small stones. In the end, he killed the enemy of his people with a single shot to the head.

While David was still young and tending the sheep, God's prophet Samuel came to David at his father's farm and anointed him as the future king of Israel. This must have sounded like a far-fetched and ridiculous idea at the time King Saul was in firm control of the entire nation of the Israelites, and he had several sons lined up to succeed him. One of them was David's best friend Jonathon later in his life.

Yet God told Samuel something incredibly interesting and powerful that people remember to this day. He said about the youth David, "Man looks on the outward appearance, but God looks on the heart…in him [David] I have found a man after My own heart." (Acts 13:22). No doubt this amazing claim influenced the young David for the rest of his life.

What does it mean to be "a man after God's own heart?" Looking closely at the triumphs and tragedies that were King David's life, we can say with certainty that it does not mean perfection like God. David at his worst was a man not to imitate. Without going into all the sordid details of the affair, he once committed adultery with another man's wife, ordered the man murdered to cover his own moral failure and to take her for his own wife, and then lied and deceived to cover his mistakes until he was confronted by one of God's prophets Nathan (II Samuel 12).

At this point though, King David showed what it meant to be the original "man after God's own heart." He repented wholeheartedly, submitted himself to God for correction, and changed his ways completely. Though the man was far from perfect in his life and reign, he always came back to the right place and attitude before God. He is a relevant inspiration to us all, as none of us are perfect.

King David at his best was a hero of a man to admire. He defeated enemies and armies with seeming ease through God's help and power. He suffered through exile and poverty in the wilderness hiding from King Saul, who later turned against him and tried repeatedly to have him killed.

When King Saul finally died, David gained control over the tribe of the Israelites (who were closely related to his family) Judah. This became the core of the Kingdom of Judah. The rest of the country (the other eleven tribes at that point, though Benjamin later joined Judah) became the Kingdom of (northern) Israel. Judah's capital was originally at Hebron. King David later moved it to Jerusalem, which has remained the capital of the country Israel to our own time today.

As king of Judah for seven and a half years, he showed himself to be a man of great compassion who hated injustice. When some opportunists killed a general of the Northern Kingdom who had come over to his side to fulfill God's promise to make him king of the two kingdoms (all Israel), David reacted to the injustice that they had committed against this general by having them put to death. He similarly treated the one who murdered the former King Saul's ruling son Ish-Bosheth for killing the innocent man on his bed while he was asleep.

The story of how David became king of Northern Israel as well as Judah is worth considering. You can see the middle-aged King David in front of the people of Israel as one of the generals of the Northern Kingdom Abner set God's plan in motion.

"Abner conferred with the elders of Israel and said, 'For some time you have wanted to make David your king. Now do it! For the Lord promised David, 'By my servant David will I rescue my people Israel from the hand of the Philistines and from the hand of all their enemies.'

Abner also spoke to the Benjamites in person. Then he went to Hebron to tell David everything that Israel and the whole tribe of Benjamin wanted to do. When Abner, who had twenty men with him, came to David at Hebron, David prepared a feast for him and his men.

Then Abner said to David, 'Let me go at once and assemble all Israel for my lord the king, so that they may make a covenant with you, and that you may rule over all that your heart desires.' So David sent Abner away, and he went in peace." (II Samuel 3:17-21).

"All the tribes of Israel came to David at Hebron and said, 'We are your own flesh and blood. In the past, while Saul was king over us, you were the one who led Israel on their military campaigns. And the Lord said to you, 'You will shepherd my people Israel, and you will become their ruler.' When all the elders of Israel had come to King David at Hebron, the king made a covenant with them at Hebron before the Lord, and they anointed David king over Israel." (II Samuel 5:1-3).

Here we see still more reasons that God called David a "man after my own heart." God saw the king as "his servant" who knew and listened to His commands. David had waited patiently for God's timing and help to become the king over both kingdoms. He did not put himself forward at the expense of his former master the old King Saul or even his children when they assumed the throne of the Northern Kingdom.

There are a lot of valuable lessons from the life of King David before you even come to his prayer (of which he wrote an entire book of them called Psalms). When he was at his best, he modeled the things that God is looking for from all of us. David loved mercy and compassion, and hated injustice. He wrote on a number of occasions about helping the poor. He worshipped God with all of his heart, soul, mind, and strength, even when his own wife made fun of him for it (reference needed please). His life is one to aspire to be like when King David was at his best.

The Prayer for Financial Salvation from King David

There are so many different prayers that you can choose from when you look at the writings of King David. Two that are closely connected are favorites of mine. They deal with salvation from troubles, especially from financial problems. The first of these is taken from Psalms 9:10:

> "Those who know your name trust in You, for you, O Lord, never forsake those who seek You."

This is a short (but so very powerful) prayer of faith in times of trouble. It gives you confidence that if you know all about the living, loving God of the universe and of mankind (I am the God of all mankind, is anything too hard for me? (Jeremiah 32:27), then you will trust Him completely.

The second part of this short prayer is the promise. You O Lord, do not abandon the ones who seek you out. Seeking God does not mean a casual prayer in between Facebook postings. There is nothing wrong with saying such a prayer, but it is not the kind of prayer that truly impresses and moves the heart of God.

Seeking God is a matter of desperation in your dire need. It often involves tears and time alone with the maker of the universe. There are countless examples through the Bible of heroes who sought God desperately like this besides King David. We will look at another two of them later in this book in the prayers of King Hezekiah and King Josiah.

Seeking God desperately is also a matter of praying without ceasing (reference needed please – "Pray without ceasing"). This means an attitude of prayer, where you are constantly asking God continuously throughout your day to help you, thanking Him for the good things He is doing for you, and asking Him to work with your struggles and mistakes despite you.

It is a radical shift in your thinking and lifestyle. Try seeking God desperately and without ceasing. You will be amazed at the way He meets you halfway if you sincerely try (I can testify to this personally).

You don't have to just take my word for it or hope it is true either. There are countless current day examples of people who have cried out to God in their desperation for help, whether it was for finances or salvation from disaster such as deathly illness. One story that I have never forgotten came from a man whose wife was diagnosed with possibly fatal cancer.

Her husband took her to the hospital for all of the treatments that they could find, hoping for the best, and needing a miracle. Meanwhile he kept busy working, taking care of the kids, cleaning the house, and trying to visit his wife as often as they could. The prognosis was grim, and as the days and weeks ticked by, she did not get better but steadily worsened. Still the man kept up with everything, sacrificing his own sleep in order to stay on top of everything.

One day while the kids were at school and he was busy trying to do all that needed to be done, getting ready for work, he suddenly reached a breaking point. He felt with certainty his wife was going to die, despite all that he had done to try to save her from the crippling cancer and to keep the family together and running as smoothly as could be expected in these dire circumstances. He stopped what he was doing.

The man threw himself on the floor of his kitchen and wept uncontrollably for his pain, her suffering, and their mutual loss. He cried out God: I just need help. I can't do it all anymore. She's going to die anyway if you don't help us. Please help us.

That was a desperate prayer to God. That was seeking God sincerely. For some combination of the reasons we have just looked at, the loving compassionate God of the universe heard his literal cries for help and extended his mighty saving arm of grace and healing to the man. When he got up, he went about his day as he had faithfully for so many months.

Suddenly his wife's condition began to improve. The doctors were astounded at the miraculous change. She grew stronger and the cancer disappeared. No one in the medical profession at the hospital could explain it. In time, she was discharged and went home, completely free of cancer. The doctors could only shrug their shoulder, smile, and shake their heads in bewilderment.

Science could not explain her recovery when the treatments had clearly failed. Years later she was still fine and without remission. That is what you call timely answer to prayer, a major miracle of God.

The husband and father knew the reason as he later testified. He had thrown himself on the floor crying, cried out to God in total exhaustion and desperation, having reached the proverbial "end of his rope." God saw him from heaven, heard his desperate cries for help, watched his sincere tears, and became moved to compassion and mercy in an otherwise hopeless situation. He has done this for me in my own life on multiple occasions, thanks to God. He will do it for you if you reach the point of really needing, wanting, and seeking His help.

King David's Related Second Prayer for Financial Help

Another so powerful prayer that moves God's heart comes from our hero King David, the original man after God's own heart. He shared it with us in Psalms again, this time in Psalms 37:23-26:

> "The Lord makes firm the steps of the one who delights in Him;
>
> though he may stumble, he will not fall,
>
> for the Lord upholds him with His hand.
>
> I was young and now I am old,
>
> Yet I have never seen the righteous forsaken
>
> Or their children begging bread.
>
> They are always generous and lend freely;
>
> Their children will be a blessing."

When you look at this mighty prayer and promise, you cannot do anything but take hope. It starts again with delighting in the Lord, showing that you are His friend who seeks Him out. You are promised that if you do this, when you stumble in your own life, you will not fall, because God himself will keep you up by his own mighty hand. This pertains to so many areas of your life, but again we are talking about finances here in particular.

King David goes on to pray and observe that in his long life (he ruled as king for forty years), he had never seen the righteous individuals abandoned by God. Their children did not go hungry or have to beg in the streets for something to eat. This is a promise from God, if you are a righteous person. A righteous individual seeks and follows God's ways as outlined in the Bible. It is a change in your attitude and lifestyle once again.

There are other characteristics of righteous people that King David mentions in the end of this prayer. This is where so many people are lacking today. The righteous are always generous to others and give or lend money to people in need freely.

It is easy to be generous with the people in your immediate family who you know and love (sometimes at least). The Bible speaks in most every book about the importance of helping the poor ("considering the poor," it calls it). Here are just a few of the many verses the Bible gives you on this topic.

> "He who has pity on the poor lends to the Lord, and He will pay back what he has given." (Proverbs 19:17).

> "He who has a generous eye will be blessed, for he gives of his bread to the poor." (Proverbs 22:9).

> "He who gives to the poor will not lack, but he who hides his eyes will have many curses." (Proverbs 28:27).

> "If you close your ears to the cry of the poor, you will cry out and you won't be heard." (Proverbs 21:13).

> "The righteous considers the cause of the poor." (Proverbs 29:7).

Each of these few examples above was written by the wisest man who ever lived--- King Solomon, the subject of our next chapter. Helping the poor is not only a sign of being a righteous person, it is more of a command than a request really if you think about what these verses say. Everyone needs to be convicted by this at some point in your own life.

If you want God to hear and answer your prayers (and especially those for financial help) like the ones King David offered for us in the beautiful examples in this chapter, you need to consider your own life. Are you helping the poor when they cry out to you for help? Or are you instead turning a blind eye and a deaf ear to their cries and going on typing a message on your Smart Phone or just generally consumed with your busy day? I will talk more about this subject in my future book, *God Hears Their Cries (You Go Do Likewise)*.

Personal Application for Your Life Today

King David knew a thing or two about serious troubles in his own life personally. Yet he could still pray and believe and testify to the faithfulness of God. The Lord saved David from personal struggles and tragic mistakes that he made, death threats from enemies, financial ruin and seeming abandonment in the wilderness, running and hiding for his very life in caves for years, and even the rebellion of (not one, but two) of his own dearly loved children.

His apparently favorite son Absalom revolted against King David in his middle age and another son Adonijah rose up against him with a band of supporters in a nearly successful coup d'état in David's old age. Both tried to take their father's throne and kill him before he died peacefully of old age. Despite his problems and troubles along the way of life, David was "a man after God's own heart."

At King David's worst, he was a failure who made terrible mistakes for which he paid the consequences in his old age. At his best, he was a person we should all aspire to be like. This is intensely personally for me, as my whole life, my mom always told me that before I was born, she felt God wanted her to name me David because I would be another "man after God's own heart."

No pressure there! Without a doubt it has dramatically impacted my life though, much as I am sure (it being spoken over him by Samuel) it influenced King David himself. On a subconscious level, I have patterned myself after my namesake King David without ever really intending to do so. What a difference it would make if we could truly say that we were people after God's own heart.

The prayers of King David could fill an entire book (and they have in

the Bible, the Psalms). We have focused here on his prayers for
financial help and rescue as they are so relevant and meaningful in
our modern lives today. In my own life, I can personally testify to the
efficacy of these prayers. For years I went to sleep every night saying
the two prayers that we looked at in this chapter:

"Those who know Your name trust in You, for You O Lord, never
forsake those who seek You" (Psalm 9:10) and

"I have been young and now am old, but I have not seen the
righteous forsaken, nor his children begging for bread." (Psalm
37:25).

I held on to these prayers especially as my own family suffered from
a financial collapse beyond our control that nearly ruined us. I talk
about this in great detail in my previous book, *God Will Never Abandon
You!* No matter how hard I worked, I could not catch up on things.

You may be able to relate to this in your own life today. Many people
have experienced troubles like these, especially in the aftermath of
the Great Recession and Global Financial Crisis. Nothing is sure
about tomorrow except that God is good all the time.

There were times when I knew that but for the grace of God we
would not survive. Yet God was faithful to keep both of these
prayer-promises to me and my family and children. I found great
peace in the midst of the turmoil and my seeming destruction
knowing that I had trusted in God and He would not abandon
(forsake) me in my dire circumstances financially.

Especially comforting was this prayer-promise that the righteous man
would not be forsaken nor his children begging for food. That
becomes very real and personal when you stand on the edge of the
proverbial precipice and stare down into the black abyss of total
collapse. In His goodness according to the words of these prayers,
God made sure that we always had a roof over our heads, food on

the table, water and electricity, and the other most critical essentials of a modern life.

This does not mean that it was always easy or painless (in particular as I was suffering equally devastating health problems at the time). It does mean that you can treat these prayers like the solid rock that they are even in your own life today. In the next chapter, our time traveling odyssey will take us on to the son of the man after God's own heart--- King Solomon, who knew very personally how faithfully God answered prayer.

4 THE PRAYER FOR WISDOM FROM KING SOLOMON

King Solomon--- the Greatest Mortal Man of Antiquity to God and Contemporaries

Leaving the original "man after God's own heart" King David behind us, our time traveling odyssey takes us next to the story and prayers of his son--- the incomparable King Solomon. Undoubtedly you have heard of this man before. As you look upon the splendor and glory of his united Kingdom of both Judah and (northern) Israel, it is impossible to not be impressed.

King Solomon was one of those most rare individuals in all of human history who had literally everything you could ask for in life. He is so easy for many of us to admire and (if we are not careful) to be envious of in fact. The greatest king of the Bible was a legend in his own time. They are still writing books about him and making films about him to this day.

You can hardly blame them looking at the man standing in front of you. He is the wealthiest man of his day on the whole earth. In his time, gold and silver were commonplace, and silver was as toys for children to play with, the book of I Kings tells us (I Kings 10:27). His trading ships ranged throughout the Eastern Mediterranean and his merchants traveled south of Egypt to the fabled King Solomon's mines. Kings and queens from around the world brought him gifts of gold, expensive spices and perfumes, and costly silks. He is splendid in every way you can possibly imagine.

Besides this, you are also impressed by his legendary wisdom. God Himself called Solomon the wisest man who had ever lived and would ever live. You can easily believe it too. Rulers of the world came from faraway places like Ethiopia to hear his renowned wisdom and to "test him with hard questions" (I Kings 10).

The Queen of Sheba (modern day Ethiopia) in particular was awed by his wisdom, the manner of his ministers, the functioning of his court, the appointments of his palaces, and the temple of God he built mostly out of costly gold and fine marble, cedar, and dressed stone. After taking it all in, she exclaimed, "Happy are your servants who sit at your feet and listen to your wisdom all day long!" (II Chronicles 9:7) in her astonishment. If that is not a testimony to glory and greatness in this world, then I do not know what is.

Solomon wrote several books in the Old Testament of the Bible like Proverbs, the Song of Solomon, and the Ecclesiastes. These are still quoted and referenced not only by believers, but by popular culture as well to this day. It is a good chance that if a person offers you some advice on any manner of topics nowadays, and quotes an old "proverb," then they are quoting the wisdom spoken and written by King Solomon. Authors still write financial advice based on Solomon's original ideas on diversification of assets and investments as one particular example.

Looking at the glory that was King Solomon (even Jesus referred to Solomon in all of his splendor and glory in one lesson he taught in Matthew 6:25-34), you can only drop your jaw at a truly golden age for the Kingdoms of Judah and Israel united. The sad news is that it was not to last for so long. Despite the long life that God blessed Solomon with, he only reigned for forty years. A single generation later, his reign would all be only a beautiful memory of the greatness and goodness of the man who God Himself loved like a son.

As you ponder the incredible sights and sounds of the court of this king, you should know that King Solomon the Magnificent was not always this person of legend whom we still talk about nearly 3,000 years later. We are now going to the early days of the man who became the mighty King Solomon to look at where his incomparable wisdom, wealth, power, and glory all came from in the first place. Prepare to go back to the relatively humble beginnings of the man who went on to become the most enduring legend of the ancient world. As you might expect by now, it all started with a simple but so incredibly powerful prayer.

King Solomon Sought God Personally and Wholeheartedly For Wisdom

Long before he became Solomon the wise and magnificent, the young king was first Solomon the humble and penitent. You can picture it as we stand there. King David had died at last. Solomon succeeded to a throne that had been beset by family struggles and bitter strife in David's old age. One of Solomon's half-brothers Adonijah had even attempted to wrest the kingdom away from their father only a few years before King David died. It was only by the grace of God that Solomon ever had the chance to become king of a united Judah and (northern) Israel.

To his undying credit, Solomon took a look around him at the great people he was going to rule. No doubt he remembered the problems his father had suffered from throughout the latter years of life. Instead of deciding to go it on his own and trust in his own abilities to be the king, Solomon did something that has intrigued people for millennia now. He sought out the God of his father David in a mighty and powerful way.

> "The king went to Gibeon to offer sacrifices, for that was the most important high place, and Solomon offered a thousand burnt offering on that altar. At Gibeon, the Lord appeared to Solomon during the night in a dream, and God said, 'Ask for whatever you want me to give you'." (I Kings 3:4-5).

This was an extremely rare and critical moment in the story of humanity. The mighty God of the universe offered this man a blank check to request whatever he wanted for himself. Ask yourself: what would you have chosen in his place?

For many people, it might be health, long life, success, wealth, fame, true love, happiness, or peace. Many of these things are not evil in and of themselves. Yet the young Solomon showed his true colors here with his response to God.

> "Solomon answered, 'You have shown great kindness to your servant, my father David, because he was faithful to you and righteous and upright in heart. You have continued this great kindness to him and have given him a son to sit on his throne this very day.
>
> Now, Lord my God, you have made your servant king in place of my father David. But I am only a little child and do not know how to carry out my duties. Your servant is here among the people you have chosen, a great people, too numerous to count or number.
>
> So give your servant a discerning heart to govern your people and to distinguish between right and wrong. For who is able to govern this great people of yours?" (I Kings 3:6-9).

Solomon surprised us all with his candid answer and humble request. He chose wisdom over the many temptations, distractions, and pleasures of this world. He also acted sacrificially and generously in requesting something for the people of his kingdoms rather than a personal favor for himself. It was the kind of selfless, divinely inspired petition that God could honor as only He can.

> "The Lord was pleased that Solomon had asked for this. So God said to him, 'Since you have asked for this and not for long life or wealth for yourself, nor have asked for the death of your enemies but for discernment in administering justice, I will do what you have asked. I will give you a wise and discerning heart, so that there will never have been anyone like you, nor will there ever be." (I Kings 3:10-12).

God granted the young king his petition with great pleasure at the request. More than this, He abundantly gave wisdom and promised

Solomon that there would not be any one either before or after him with his understanding. If the story stopped here, it would have been worth remembering for all time. But God has a way of honoring our prayers that we offer up in generosity and selflessness way beyond our expectations.

> "Moreover, I will give you what you have not asked for--- both wealth and honor--- so that in your lifetime you will have no equal among kings. And if you walk in obedience to me a and keep my decrees and commands as David your father did, I will give you a long life.

> Then Solomon awoke--- and he realized it had been a dream. He returned to Jerusalem, stood before the ark of the Lord's covenant and sacrificed burnt offerings and fellowship offerings. Then he gave a feast for all his court." (I Kings 3:13-15).

The irony in all of this of course is that by not asking for one thing for himself, King Solomon received from God all of the important things he might have requested. He had an unequalled wisdom for all time, a wealth that would be inexhaustible and incomparable for his entire life, He would receive honor and glory to which no one could compare in his days. Just to sweeten the deal, God offered Solomon a long life as well in exchange for honoring and obeying Him. My friends, it does not get any better than this.

We Learn So Much From Solomon's Dream Prayer for Wisdom

This particular prayer of King Solomon is such a powerful example to us of how we should be praying in our own modern-day lives as well. There are several great takeaway lessons from this petition to God.

1. King Solomon asked humbly by calling his father (and himself) God's servant.

2. The king remembered who He was dealing with and praised and honored God as He deserves. It is all too easy to skip over this important part of prayer in the desperation of our personal needs.

3. Solomon asked for something that deeply touched the heart of the king of the universe Himself. He requested wisdom and discernment to govern his people. God honors requests for wisdom in hard situations especially as the God who "gives generously to all men who ask Him." (James 1:5)

4. The king asked sacrificially by putting aside all of his own desires personally to ask for wise counsel in governing the nation. Can you say that you would do the same if God appeared to you with such an incredible offer?

5. Solomon asked in great faith, believing that he would get what he was asking for from God.

6. The young king acknowledged his own inability to meet the needs and do the job alone, instead choosing to credit God as the only being who had the necessary ability to rule the people.

7. King Solomon sought out God on a lonely mountaintop wilderness where there were no distractions available, like today's Internet, cable television, smart phones, Facebook, girls or guys, and more. The Bible tells one story after another about how people encountered Him personally by going out into the wilderness to seek him.

Personal Application for Your Life Today

On this last point, there is a parallel modern-day story reinforcing this idea that this particular prayer is not merely a one-off miracle intended for just the young King Solomon. About a hundred years ago, a young Jewish rabbi in New York City was just opening up a house of worship in the city. He wanted to see it succeed and touch people from all around the area, so he started at the right place, modeling his life on King Solomon.

The rabbi went off into the woods of upper state New York to find God like his people's greatest king did almost 3,000 years ago. He went alone and made camp in the wilderness like Solomon. For three days, the man prayed and waited on God. He encountered Him personally here.

At the end of his spiritual retreat in the wilderness, he came back to the city supercharged and filled with God's power and presence in his own life. The new Jewish house of worship was a huge success. In no time at all, its fame had spread throughout the Big Apple. People came from all over the area to experience its outreach for themselves.

Eventually the now old rabbi died and his son took over the house of worship and all that went along with it. He decided that in honor of his father's greatest story, he ought to go back to those woods where the old man had met with God. So the son of the first rabbi went out and spent a day camping in the same forest.

Only he did not seek God deeply and fervently for himself. Instead, he pondered the memory and vision of his father and how he had encountered God personally on that very spot. At the end of his day and night in the wilderness, he decided that it was enough.

The son of the great deceased rabbi then went home and took over the family house of worship. Throughout his time as the rabbi, the center did alright, but it seemed to lack the vitality, excitement, and effectiveness that it had shown under the leadership and guidance of the old rabbi. No one could put his finger on why at the time, and so time passed and the attendance leveled off then began to slowly decline. Finally the day came when the great rabbi's son also died.

His son, the grandson of the great rabbi, then took over the family-run house of worship. Before he started his own outreach and ministry, he remembered fondly the stories that his grandfather had told him with such enthusiasm and passion about meeting God in the wilderness (of upstate New York) like their ancestor King Solomon.

The grandson third generation rabbi considered what he should do. He contemplated going out to visit the holy ground where his grandpa had met with God and his father had gone to commemorate the event.

But this new rabbi's life was too busy, and camping out did not really appeal to him. He needed to pick up the reigns of the worship center and move forward. So instead, he set aside an afternoon one day and spent a few hours pondering the meaning of his grandfather's time and vision with God. Then he decided that it was enough.

A few years later, the wonderful and effective Jewish house of worship that had been the talk of New York City was in full decline. Eventually the people stopped coming altogether and then it closed for good. All that remained was a legacy started by the grandfather, one man who decided that the example and prayer of King Solomon was important enough to imitate it in his own modern life.

There are so many different lessons in this true story that it is hard to know where to start. Taking time to get away from the distractions of your life to be with God is the best thing you can possibly do if you want to have your prayers answered. Better than this though, getting out into the wilderness is a time-honored tradition (in both Judaism and Christianity) for meeting with the Author of the universe. Solomon did it, and Elijah and Moses did as well. Jesus followed their examples, as did Peter and John, and eventually Paul in the book of Acts after them. There is something about finding God in the wilderness.

If you need wisdom, the Bible actually encourages you to ask God for it, saying that He gives liberally to all men who do. (James 1:5). In the difficult, dangerous, and most distracting in history times that we live in now, which of us does not need wisdom from God? You need to know what to do with your life, how to take care of your family, and how to avoid disasters along the way.

I can only encourage you by sharing that in my own life I have found the example set so famously by Solomon to be incredibly powerful and real. If you go out to a quiet place surrounded by the beauty of God's glorious creation, escape from the petty distractions of your own daily life that keep you from reaching out to and hearing from Him, and earnestly ask Him for the wisdom He already promised to give you generously, then you will find Him and the answers to the difficult questions that you seek.

What will you choose to ask God for then? Will it be something noble and sacrificial like how you can help hurting, lost people or positively impact the world for the glory of God? These are the prayers that move the heart of God most. Consider the example of the wisest man who ever lived from three millennia ago. King Solomon chose to ask God for wisdom and discernment. The world has never been the same since.

5 THE PRAYER FOR DELIVERNCE FROM KING JEHOSHAPHAT

You climb thoughtfully back into the time traveling odyssey as we leave the glory and splendor that was the life and reign of King Solomon. Our next stop takes us nearly 60 years later (and past three more Kings of Judah) to the reign of good King Jehoshaphat. You can see him there as he leads his people of the now much smaller kingdom (since the golden age of Solomon has faded into the mists) forward with the Lord "God of their fathers." He is a king with whom God is pleased.

This does not mean that his life and times are easy though. Major changes have befallen the Kingdom of Judah since the glorious age of Solomon ended, forever beyond hope of recall. King Jehoshaphat is a good and God fearing man. He does what is right in the eyes of the Lord (most of the time).

Yet they have very real and pressing problems in Jehoshaphat's Judah (as you will too in your own life, no matter how good and obediently you choose to live your life with God). Gone are the great and powerful, victorious armies of King David the heroic "man after God's own heart." Lost is the wisdom of King Solomon that helped the United Kingdoms of Judah and Northern Israel to become a regional superpower in his day. The horses, chariots, and armies of Solomon are also gone.

The newer smaller Kingdom of Judah is tiny. You can see Jehoshaphat's little kingdom and you fear for its safety. It is only two of the twelve tribes of the ancient Israelites (Judah and Benjamin), Jerusalem, Lachish, and a handful of other cities plus their towns and villages (it is not so much bigger than the modern-day country of Malta and Gozo that I call home).

As you ponder what has happened to reduce the size of the Kingdom of Judah to a fraction of its previous boundaries, you realize that kings after Solomon made choices and they had consequences. The son of the great Solomon, Rehoboam, chose poorly. He would not listen to the people of the united two kingdoms Israel and Judah when they asked him to reduce the heavy burdens that Solomon had placed on them in taxation and labor requirements.

The result led to the final breakup of the two kingdoms. The United Kingdom of Israel and Judah would never come back again. Judah had a huge asset though. It held King David and Solomon's special capital of Jerusalem where they had built God's temple.

It makes you sad as you ponder all of this, but then you turn your eyes again to the current troubles that King Jehoshaphat and his Kingdom of Judah are facing. You focus on the crisis unfolding in front of you. Despite having served and followed God faithfully, King Jehoshaphat experienced trouble in his own life and in those of his people. You can relate to this as you watch the scene before you.

They had done nothing wrong. You might say that this was a test from God to see if they trusted Him now that their armies, glory, wealth, and power were forever gone. You will encounter such tests in your own life too. I have myself, and from personal experience I can tell you that they are not always painless Yet God is still good all of the time, even when life hurts, even when it is hard, and even when it is painful.

The crisis situation that faced King Jehoshaphat and the people of the Kingdom of Judah was this. A great horde of allied armies from the East had banded together to attack the Kingdom of Judah. It reads like an adventure story from a modern day movie, as told in the Second Chronicles of the Kings of Judah.

> "After this the Moabites and Ammonites, and with them some of the Meunites, came against Jehoshaphat for battle. Some men came and told Jehoshaphat, "A great multitude is coming against you from Edom [modern day Jordan], from beyond the sea; and behold they are in Hazazon-tamar (that is, Engedi).
>
> Then Jehoshaphat was afraid and set his face to seek the

Lord, and proclaimed a fast throughout all Judah. And Judah assembled to seek help from the Lord, from all the cities of Judah they came to seek the Lord." (II Chronicles 20:1-4, English Standard Version).

You can understand completely why the hero of our story King Jehoshaphat is afraid. Yet his response to the natural fear of a hopeless situation was crucial. Jehoshaphat turned his heart, mind, and soul to seek the Lord for help. He did not blame God or become angry with Him in his circumstances because "life got too hard." There is a great lesson in this good man's immediate response for all of us. It explains why his subsequent prayer was so powerful.

> "And Jehoshaphat stood in the assembly of Judah and Jerusalem, in the house of the Lord, before the new court, and said, 'O Lord, God of our fathers, are you not God in heaven? You rule over all the kingdoms of the nations. In your hand are power and might, so that none is able to withstand you. Did you not, our God, drive out the inhabitants of this land before your people Israel, and give it forever to the descendants of Abraham your friend?

> And they have lived In it and have built for you in it a sanctuary for your name, saying, 'If disaster comes upon us, the sword, judgment, or pestilence, or famine, we will stand before this house and before you—for your name is in this house—and cry out to you in our affliction, and you will hear and save. And now behold, the men of Ammon and Moab and Mount Seir, whom you would not let Israel invade when they came from the land of Egypt, and whom they avoided and did not destroy—behold they reward us by coming to drive us out of your possession, which you have given us to inherit.

> O our God, will you not execute judgment on them? **For we are powerless against this great horde that is coming**

against us. We do not know what to do, but our eyes are on you." (II Chronicles 20:8-12, English Standard Version).

Now that is what you call a super-powerful and model prayer. It has all the right elements in it. Jehoshaphat gives praise and thanks to God, reminds God of His promises, lays out his urgent needs, admits his inability to save himself (and his kingdom and people) on his own, and then effectively appeals for and waits for help. The pure and simplest essence of the prayer of Jehoshaphat comes down to the last line: **"We do not know what to do, but our eyes are on you."**

God Saves Jehoshaphat and the Kingdom of Judah From Destruction

Now we come to the exciting part of this amazing true story. Did God answer and save his man King Jehoshaphat and the people of the Kingdom of Judah from imminent destruction at the hands of this horde from the East? Take a look.

> "Meanwhile all Judah stood before the Lord, with their little ones, their wives, and their children. And the Spirit of the Lord came upon Jahaziel the son of Zechariah... in the midst of the assembly. And he said, 'Listen, all Judah and inhabitants of Jerusalem and King Jehoshaphat. Thus says the Lord to you, 'Do not be afraid and do not be dismayed at this great horde. For the battle is not yours but God's. Tomorrow go down against them. Behold, they will come up by the ascent of Ziz. You will find them at the end of the valley, east of the wilderness of Jeruel. You will not need to fight this battle. Stand firm, hold your position, and see the salvation of the Lord on your behalf, O Judah and Jerusalem.' Do not be afraid and do not be dismayed. Tomorrow go out against them, and the Lord will be with you." (II Chronicles 20:13-17 English Standard Version).

That was it! God just answered the powerful prayer of King Jehoshaphat right there in the middle of the assembly as all the people prayed. They sought out God in their desperation and earnestness, and He gave them hope and a promise that they would not even have to fight the horde from the East.

> "Then Jehoshaphat bowed his head with his face to the ground, and all Judah and the inhabitants of Jerusalem fell down before the Lord, worshipping the Lord...And they rose early in the morning and went out into the wilderness of Tekoa.
>
> And when they went out, Jehoshaphat stood and said, 'Hear me, Judah and inhabitants of Jerusalem! Believe in the Lord your God, and you will be established; believe His prophets, and you will succeed.'
>
> And when he had taken counsel with the people, he appointed those who were to sing to the Lord and praise him in holy attire, as they went before the army and say, 'Give thanks to the Lord, for His steadfast love endures forever'."
> (II Chronicles 20:18-21, English Standard Version).

Now Jehoshaphat and the people are still waiting to see their prayer be answered literally. They already have a promise from God that He will help them. Now while they are faithfully following through on God's instructions to them, they go rejoicing and singing praises.

This is a leader and his people who believe in the power of God. They have not yet seen the deliverance, yet they know that it is coming. Their prayers are more powerful because of their faith and trust in God. This is a mighty and moving lesson for all of us in our own lives today.

> "And when they began to sing and praise, the Lord set an ambush against the men of Ammon, Moab, and Mount Seir,

who had come against Judah, so that they were routed. For the men of Ammon and Moab rose against the inhabitants of Mount Seir, devoting them to destruction, and when they had made an end of the inhabitants of Seir, they all helped to destroy one another.

When Judah came to the watchtower of the wilderness, they looked toward the horde, and behold, there were dead bodies lying on the ground; none had escaped. When Jehoshaphat and his people came to take their spoil, they found among them, in great numbers, goods, clothing, and precious things, which they took for themselves until they could carry no more. They were three days in taking the spoil, it was so much. On the fourth day they assembled in the Valley of Beracah, for there they blessed the Lord...

Then they returned, every man of Judah and Jerusalem, and Jehoshaphat at their head returning to Jerusalem, for the Lord had made them to rejoice over their enemies. They came to Jerusalem with harps and lyres and trumpets, to the house of the Lord.

And the fear of God came on all the kingdoms of the countries when they heard that the Lord had fought against the enemies of Israel. So the realm of Jehoshaphat was quiet, for his God gave him rest all around." (II Chronicles 20:22-30, English Standard Version).

The amazing result of this incredible victory should give you chills. God delivered a man who trusted in Him and saved the people who followed alongside the king. Jehoshaphat and the people received deliverance from hopelessness and fear. Through their trust and obedience, God got all of the glory for the victory, so that even the surrounding nations came to respect the power and might of the Lord God of the universe and of all mankind.

Personal Application for Your Life Today

There is so very much for us today in this incredible true story of the successful triumph of Jehoshaphat and the people of the Kingdom of Judah over their hopeless-looking circumstances. Like you might expect, the initial reaction from the king was fear. His circumstances were greater than he could possibly overcome on his own. Then Jehoshaphat and his people turned their face to seek God in desperation. Without deliverance from their troubles, they were finished. They knew it and admitted it.

You feel like this in your own life today. I have felt that way personally in mine on many occasions between my recurring health problems of the past, financial troubles, and other personal struggles at home. I can hear you saying it now: the answers seem so simple when you read this powerful, moving, true story and prayer of King Jehoshaphat and the people of Judah. That is because they actually are simple!

Here is their five step method to success:

1. They sought God and then trusted Him completely in their dire need and fear.
2. The king and his people carried out God's instructions (from promises that we now have in the Bible).
3. God promised to fight their struggle for them, so that all they had to do was go in faith to the site of the battle.
4. They just showed up--- believing, trusting, and praising and thanking God for the deliverance that was coming.
5. When they arrived, they found out that God had already delivered them as He promised, *before they even got there.*

The Bible repeatedly tells us that "in our weakness He is strong," (II Corinthians 12:9) and that "You dear children are from God and have overcome them because the One who is in you is greater than the one who is in the world." (I John 4:4). "No weapon formed against you shall prosper."(Isaiah 54:17). "God has not given you a spirit of fear, but he has given unto you a spirit of power, a spirit of love, and of a sound, good mind." (II Timothy 1:7). Do not be afraid! You are an overcomer! Deliverance is available for you in your own life today if you only ask God for it.

If you say this amazing and simple prayer with faith and trust in God, He can and will do the same personal miracles for you (as he did for Jehoshaphat and the people of Judah). **"I do not know what to do, but my eyes are on You."**

Pray it like you mean it, like your whole life depends on it being true. This makes all the difference in the world. This matters to God. It reshaped the hopeless-looking future of the kingdom of Judah. It will do the same for you today.

6 THE PRAYER FOR PURPOSE FROM ISAIAH THE PROPHET

Next our time traveling odyssey takes us forward in time a few generations in the story of the Kingdom of Judah. One hundred and fifteen years have now passed since you left the reign and realm of the great and Godly King Jehoshaphat, a real mighty man of valor who knew that his strength lay in the Lord His God. You step out of our time machine and look around you, wondering how the kingdom has changed.

In front of you stands a man. He is not a king. He is a commoner. His name is Isaiah. As you watch him, you see that there is something extraordinary about him. Isaiah has just received a vision from the almighty God. He looks almost overwhelmed by the magnitude of it.

The man has the look on his face of one who has just seen the glory of the Lord God of the universe literally in front of him, yet lived to tell about it. Isaiah has been called by God to be His prophet (or messenger) to the people and to four kings of the Kingdom of Judah.

You can see and feel his vision too as it unfold in front of you. It is a moving and powerful glimpse of how he will be used to change the fate of this nation of God's people. Isaiah is touched deeply by it, and realizes that he will spend his whole life on a quest to find the ultimate Godly, warrior-king of the Kingdom of Judah. It all started with the first and sixth chapters of the self-titled Book of Isaiah and with a simple yet powerful prayer that changed the world forever.

> "The vision concerning Judah and Jerusalem that Isaiah son of Amoz saw during the reigns of Uzziah, Jotham, Ahaz, and Hezekiah, kings of Judah. Hear me, you heavens! Listen, earth! For the Lord has spoken: 'I reared children and brought them up, but they have rebelled against me. The ox knows its master, the donkey its owner's manger, but Israel does not know, my people do not understand'." (Isaiah 1)

You can already see how things are changing in the exciting Kingdom of Judah (and not for the better) since the death of King Jehoshaphat in the last chapter. The nation has begun to turn away from the God of its fathers. Yet here comes Isaiah exploding onto the scene. Things are about to change for the much better. The vision he sees in his head is stunning and will send chills up your spine as you witness it.

> "In the year that King Uzziah died, I saw the Lord, high and exalted, seated on a throne; and the train of His robe filled the temple. Above him were seraphim, each with six wings:

With two wings they covered their faces, with two they covered their feet, and with two they were flying. And they were calling to one another:

'Holy, holy, holy is the Lord Almighty; the whole earth is full of his glory.' At the sound of their voices the doorposts and thresholds shook and the temple was filled with smoke.

'Woe to me!' I cried. 'I am ruined! For I am a man of unclean lips, and I live among a people of unclean lips, and my eyes have seen the King, the Lord Almighty.'

Then one of the seraphim flew to me with a live coal in his hand, which he had taken with tongs from the altar. With it he touched my mouth and said, 'See this has touched your lips; your guilt is taken away and your sin [mistakes] atoned for'." (Isaiah 6:1-7)

Put yourself in this extraordinary individual's shoes for a few minutes as you watch him and this powerful vision from God envelop him. This is a man from the Kingdom of Judah, one of God's people the Jews whom He called hundreds of years earlier and for whom he worked enormous miracles over the centuries. Isaiah is certainly a Godly man, or he would not have experienced such a vision from God in the first place. At the time, it was common for people who had seen God and all of His glory to die from the full on power and impact of it.

Isaiah actually saw heaven and the temple and the glory of God and His court all around Him. It was overwhelming and moving. How many people in all of human history can make such a claim, to have literally experienced a glimpse of the supernatural, of God the ruler of the universe in His heaven?

You can feel Isaiah trembling with excitement in front of you. But the best is yet to come. Isaiah is about to show his true mettle and reveal his inner heart before you. And we know that "man looks on the outward appearance, but God looks on the heart." (I Samuel 16:7).

> "Then I heard the voice of the Lord saying 'Whom shall I send? And who will go for us?'
>
> And I said, '**Here am I. Send me!**'" (Isaiah 6:8).

That was the divine moment for our rising hero Isaiah the prophet. Roughly 700 years before the birth of Jesus Christ, the man has just uttered a phrase that changed not only the fate of the Kingdom of Judah for generations to come, but that will change your life forever too. It all began with one brief statement of faith, a powerful but simple, single- line prayer.

"I am here; I am willing; I will go. Lord send me!" The exclamation point in this powerful prayer from Isaiah and the Kingdom of Judah speaks volumes as to the excitement and enthusiasm from a man whose entire life has just been transformed right before your eyes. The God of the universe who rules the heavens and made all the earth has just reached out.

God touched the fate of one man who responded with his willingness to serve the great and mighty Lord God in his own life. It is a defining moment in the life of Isaiah and human history. It can be the same life-changing moment for you personally if you believe this powerful prayer today and say it from your heart to God: "I am here; I am willing; I will go. Lord send me!"

God Answers this Prayer So Powerfully for Isaiah

You have seen and heard Isaiah utter a prayer that moved the heart of God in his own day and age. It still moves God's heart today. How did God respond to Isaiah's willingness to go and be an instrument and a messenger to a darkening world? He poured out such a mighty calling and purpose in Isaiah's life that the man would never be the same.

Did God honor this prayer in Isaiah's life? You can see him standing there before you, and his life is an exciting one— full of purpose, power, and meaning. This does not mean that it was always easy. Isaiah actually had some hard times along the road in his walk down the path that God gave him in response to the enthusiastic prayer from his heart.

God loved Isaiah's willingness, so He gave him mission after mission to the reigns of four different Kings of Judah, the rulers of Isaiah's country, day, and age. Just take a look at some of the many powerful things that Isaiah was used to do during his time of outreach as the prophet to the nation of Judah:

> "Then Isaiah said, 'Hear now, you house of David! Is it not enough to try the patience of humans? Will you try the patience of my God also? (Isaiah 7:13).

> "He [King Hezekiah] sent Eliakim the palace administrator, Shebna the secretary, and the leading priests, all wearing sackcloth, to the prophet Isaiah son of Amoz. (II Kings 19:2)

> "King Hezekiah and the prophet Isaiah son of Amoz cried out in prayer to heaven about this." (II Chronicles 32:20).

> "Isaiah said to them, 'Tell your master, 'This is what the Lord says: Do not be afraid of what you have heard—those words with which the underlings of the king of Assyria have blasphemed Me'." (II Kings 19:6).

> "Then Isaiah son of Amoz sent a message to Hezekiah: 'This is what the Lord, the God of Israel, says: 'I have heard your prayer concerning Sennacherib king of Assyria'." (II Kings 19:20).

> "Then the prophet Isaiah called on the Lord, and the Lord

made the shadow go back the ten steps [ten hours back in time] it had gone down on the stairway of Ahaz." (II Kings 20:11).

"Then Isaiah the prophet wen to King Hezekiah and asked, 'What did those men say, and where did they come from'? 'From a distant land,' Hezekiah replied. 'They came from Babylon'." (II Kings 20:14).

"Then Isaiah said to Hezekiah, 'Hear the word of the Lord'." (II Kings 20:16)

"The other events of Hezekiah's reign and his acts of devotion are written in the vision of the prophet Isaiah son of Amoz in the book of the kings of Judah and Israel." (II Chronicles 32:32).

"The other events of Uzziah's reign, from beginning to end, are recorded by the prophet Isaiah son of Amoz." (II Chronicles 26:22).

"A prophecy against Babylon that Isaiah son of Amoz saw…" (Isaiah 13:1).

Isaiah wrote the first 39 chapters of the book named after him. Besides this and most importantly, Isaiah was used by God to prophesy and predict the coming into the world of the Messiah Jesus Christ, the Son of God (around 700 years after he prophesied this).

This man Isaiah was on a quest, a mission if you will. He spent the rest of his life looking for "God's righteous man" (to be the ruler of the tiny kingdom that God called His own). Isaiah would find such a valiant man in the person of King Hezekiah, a real-life hero of the Kingdom of Judah and of the faith. We will meet him in the next chapter.

Personal Application for Your Life Today

I've said it before in my last book on prayer— _The Three Miraculous Prayers of King Hezekiah: A Good Man's Example for Our Own Troubled Times_: one man can make a difference. This is more than a clever slogan from the hit 1980's television series "Knight Rider" (starring David Hasselhoff). It is the absolute truth that mattered in the life and times of Isaiah the prophet of the Kingdom of Judah. It matters for you own life today still.

Don't we all need purpose in our lives? Praying the simple prayer from Isaiah's calling will make all the difference in your own life. For me personally, for years I have said this prayer at night before I go to bed and in the mornings when I get up (not every single day, but often enough).

God has richly honored this prayer in my own life (so that I can testify about it to you here) as He raises me up to take these words of hope and messages of encouragement to the churches, to small groups, and to individuals I have met with in the past (and who I meet everywhere--- in the streets, on trips, while traveling to speak about the books and do radio interviews) in America, Europe, and Great Britain.

I don't share this to boast. It is merely an encouraging testimony from me to you about the things that God can (and will) do with and in your own life if only you pray this simple but powerful prayer to Him and mean it in your own heart:

"I am here, I am willing, I will go, Lord choose me, Lord send me, Lord use me" based on the prayer of Isaiah.

This is a prayer that He truly loves to honor. It is a prayer that will change your life for the better and give you daily hope, purpose, and meaning. It is a so-powerful one that I can tell you has absolutely made all the difference in the world for me personally. It will for you too.

7 THE PRAYER FOR DELIVERNCE FROM KING HEZEKIAH

It is only fitting as you climb back into the Odyssey still thoughtful about what you saw and learned about Isaiah the prophet that the next stop in this time traveling adventure through the Kingdom of Judah is the life and reign of King Hezekiah. If this amazing man who you can only stare at in front of you was a super hero today, he would be Captain America, God's righteous man.

In fact as you look closely at him, you can see why God said about him that "Among the kings of Judah, there was none like him before or after." (II Kings 18:5). It seems that King Hezekiah, who has led an extraordinary life of power and miracles for fifteen years has become ill. The more you look at him, the more you see that he is dying before his time. This good, Godly, great man is sick from a wasting illness. He lies on a bed and has just finished a conversation with our hero Isaiah the prophet from the last chapter.

You can hear every word they are saying. Isaiah has just told King Hezekiah that he must get his house in order now, as God's righteous man is not going to recover from this illness. It brings tears to your eyes as you hear Isaiah somberly and grimly tell "God's servant" King Hezekiah that he will die from this horrible wasting illness.

> "The prophet Isaiah son of Amoz went to him and said, 'This is what the Lord says: Put your house in order, because you are going to die; you will not recover." (II Kings 20:1).

1 Hezekiah Dying from a wasting illness asks God for a sign of healing

I have said it before in my first book on prayer (*The Three Miraculous Prayers of King Hezekiah – A Good Man's Example for Our Own Troubled Times*), and I will say it again. It does not matter how close you are to God in your life, if someone gives you a pronunciation that you will die within days, you will at the very least be a little bit nervous. This is human nature, and none of us are immune to fears, doubts, and even a little worry about what will happen to us when we die. Naturally "God's righteous man" was nervous too. Yet one of the most amazing things about this great, good man you see lying there before you is that he never surrendered and never wavered in his faith.

Instead, King Hezekiah chose to do the greatest thing that any superhero of the faith can do. He called upon the secret super power that God gave us all today in such true stories as this one. He turned to face the wall and uttered this amazing prayer that still works miraculous wonders for people to this day.

> "Hezekiah turned his face to the wall and prayed to the Lord. 'Remember, Lord, how I have walked before you faithfully and with wholehearted devotion and have done what is good in your eyes.' And Hezekiah wept bitterly." (II Kings 20:2-3).

As you watch what happens to this once-mighty hero of man next, you feel the tears welling up in your eyes. You can't help it, this is such a moving scene and it reminds you of past and present pain and illness in your own life and in the lives of your own loved ones.

> "Before Isaiah had left the middle court, the word of the Lord came to him: Go back and tell Hezekiah, the rule of my people, 'This is what the Lord, the God of your father David, says, 'I have heard your prayer and seen your tears; I will heal you. On the third day from now you will go up to the temple of the Lord. I will add fifteen years to your life. And I will deliver you and this city from the hand of the king of Assyria. I will defend this city for my sake and for the sake of my servant David.' Then Isaiah said, 'Prepare a poultice of figs.'

They did so and applied it to the boil, and he [Hezekiah] recovered." (II Kings 20:4-7).

This is one of the most amazing stories of healing that has ever been told, in the Bible as well as all of human history. It is a prayer so powerful that it shook the whole world. It is a moving cry to God that you can and should use in your own life. "I have walked faithfully and loyally before you my whole life…"

I have said it before, and I will say it again. Not everyone has this testimony like King Hezekiah in his or her own life. Maybe you have been a child of God since you were only a kid. Maybe you have not. You could have a mighty testimony to share with the world of all the many things from which God saved you in your own life. The prayer of King Hezekiah is not only powerful for those who have led an exemplary life since the days of their youth. The activating secret power in the prayer was the fact that the great king wept bitterly before the Lord.

This does not mean that he was bitter about his circumstances. King Hezekiah would not have seen this enormous miracle of fantastic and life-changing healing if he had been angry at God! As hard as it may seem in your own dire circumstances where your health is failing, you have to hold on to God. Turning against Him only cuts you off from the "God of all mankind." He is the only one who can save you in the end.

Personal Application for Your Life

I have some personal experience in this arena about suffering from a wasting ailment like King Hezekiah. Glory to God I can say today that He saved my life as he did the good king's over 2,500 years ago. Here is the testimony that God gave me to share with you and all the world after I lived a life, "faithfully and loyally before God" like the king. I hope that it will encourage you in your own suffering and pain, wherever you are in your life and health today.

My life is a living testimony to the power of God as He worked it through King Hezekiah so many years ago. I became desperately ill back in 2014. I was hospitalized two different times because of my own strange "wasting illness" that I contracted immediately after the amazing book and radio tour all around the state of Florida with *The Three Miraculous Prayers of King Hezekiah*.

When I was nearing the conclusion of doing book signings in the bookstores and radio station interviews in December of 2013, we went to this huge Lifeway Christian Store. We ended the book tour on a high note with about 50 people (who had heard the interview on the Christian radio station) there in Tallahassee coming out to meet me and to encourage each other with the exciting book. God was good and the bookstore sold all 30 copies of the books which they had ordered in for the event.

One woman came up to me at the table and gave me what is still my greatest testimonial on my writing there. She walked up to me (not knowing me), had heard the radio interview, had not read all of the book yet, and then said these encouraging words that have kept me going with my Christian book writing for years: "The Holy Spirit wanted me to tell you that you write beautifully and to thank you for retelling this powerful and moving story for us" (that's the *Three Miraculous Prayers of King Hezekiah*. To this day it remains a book where God is reaching out and touching people's heart around the world (across the U.S., Canada, Europe, and Great Britain; online, in bookstores, in hardback, in paperback, in Kindle format, in Nook book e-book format, across every channel. I am humbled by what God continues to do with this story of his greatest Old Testament hero King Hezekiah).

Now after I finished that amazing book promotion, and within two months of leaving that mountain top experience with God, I became horribly sick from a "wasting illness." I was twice in the hospital. I nearly died in a car wreck trying to get to a pharmacy for medicine one day. I was alone at home with my then-infant son Alex trying to work and take care of him like that in this humiliating condition for 10 long months.

No one could help me. The doctors did all kinds of tests on my body, everything imaginable. They could not figure out what to do or how to help me. My sleep was completely destroyed I was so sick. I used to lie in bed for 10-12 hours at night, shaking, sweating, and trembling and crying myself finally to sleep (for only 2 hours) until I would wake up again the next morning and start it all over again. Everything I ate ran through me. Enough said.

I drank gallons of Gatorade and PowerAde in a desperate battle against dehydration. I consumed countless boxes of Imodium over the next year. I was still hospitalized twice for dehydration; nothing would stick inside me that I ate. I lost weight as I gradually almost stopped eating in a desperate bid to stop what felt to me like dysentery.

No doctors could figure it out. My boss at the time offered to fly me to Houston for some of the best medical care in the United States, as he was worried about me dying without help. He did not offer to pay for the medical treatment, and as I had no good health insurance at the time, I cried in my despair and pain. I could not afford to go and be saved.

No one could help me. I suffered from migraine headaches that felt like my head was being squeezed in a vice. I experience sudden radical blood pressure spikes on a regular basis that shot up to over 200/110. My beloved parents were so worried about me that they sold their house where they had lived happily for about 15 years and moved to Ocala to try to help me, renting an apartment in our apartment complex neighborhood.

My poor dad who was dying from Alzheimer's at the time would come every day and sit and play with little two year old Alex to bring some joy into the little boy's life while his poor daddy whom he (and his five year old sister, my daughter Irina) loved so dearly would lie down on my work lunch break. We would like down together every day at his nap time. It was only because I worked a computer and Internet job at the time that I could keep working at all.

Whatever money we had left saved was consumed that year in medicines, health supplements, doctor visits, hospital visits, and growing Gatorade bills. I got so sick and so bad that I remember walking five minutes to Publix (our big Tesco-styled grocery store in the Southeastern U.S.). No one would trust me to drive anymore. I had nearly killed myself once trying to do so because I was gradually becoming brain dead from lack of sleep over a protracted period of many months. I forgot to buckle little Alex's car seat seatbelt as I could not focus.

So I would walk to the grocery store and spend upwards of an hour starting at the vitamin and natural remedy sections, praying God to show me something, to save me. I was too sick to go to church for more than 6 months.

I reached a point where I could barely read anymore from exhaustion. You can only imagine how hard this is for someone whose passions in life include reading and writing! My kids would cry for and over me as they saw me lying sick on the couch.

We went out to dinner one night together when I was feeling a little better. I was pale as a ghost. I spilled my drink on the dinner table that night and ruined the evening for everyone. I could not help it; I shook so badly at that point. I was so sick and so shaking and so exhausted and weak, that finally I realized I was going to die.

I used to lie trembling in the bed at night, praying to God, "I'm going to die from this horrible illness that no one can diagnose if You don't help me. How ironic that I wrote a book about King Hezekiah and his wasting illness, when I was exactly the same age that he was when he got sick (we were both 39), and now I'm going to die from an unknown ailment if You don't help me. I am wasting away just like he did God. Who will take care of my poor children? They cry for me every day and night. They love me; they need me. When you require my life from me, I will go home to heaven and not fight it. But please not today God, not without anyone else to pray for these children, to take them to church, to teach them about You, to take care of them physically and financially, to even take them to school every day!"

It seemed like God had heard (we know that He had) and was helping me, as I experienced a brief recovery. After this respite in my own wasting illness for a few weeks, I worsened. I suffered a second bout of it. They performed a colonoscopy on me and came back with nothing significant enough to cause me such problems as the dysentery-like condition that I continued to suffer from. They checked me for exotic parasites. It all came back negative. The doctors shrugged their shoulders and finally wrote me off as a hopeless and un-diagnosable case.

After the medical profession failed me, at that point I reached a new low. I prayed to God, "I want to come Home to you Lord. I have nothing left to give. Please take care of my children for me. Please take me home. I can't do this anymore. I'm spent. Please just take me home."

I look back on my life nearly five years ago and think how ironic it actually was that I wanted to be that great, good man King Hezekiah, and told God that. There is a lesson in such a prayer somewhere--- be careful what you wish for, they say!

Yet God honored that prayer in my life in positive ways too. I have seen huge and amazing miracles personally after that low point. He raised me up off of my sick bed, and saved me from my death bed, (as I had honored the poor like the Bible strongly recommends in Psalm 41:1-4), and He heard my cries for desperate help. I did not die!

The same way the wasting illness hit me out of seemingly nowhere, it simply vanished over a period of about a month. Here is something i have not previously told many people. The wasting illness seemed to suddenly leave me when Anna and I made the decision to go back to live in Europe, back to Malta before I died. I wanted to be back on God's little island nation in the Mediterranean Sea. I had felt good there and served Him faithfully, and I thought that maybe He would help me if we moved back there. It was all part of God's own good plan, in his own perfect timing, though it was far from easy or painless for me at the time.

The moment we made that life-changing choice (we have remained living in Malta in Europe ever since), it was like someone had poured a medicinal tonic over my whole body. Within days the dysentery-like condition began to improve. I gradually grew stronger. I was able to eat again. I stopped losing weight. My sleep became healed. My body grew stronger day by day. It took me fully two months to make a complete recovery. That is how sick I had been, that is how close to dying alone at home (with only sweet little Alex around me during the days) I actually came.

I realized powerfully on a few dramatic occasions that only God in His mercy and goodness had kept me alive. He saved me. He worked a miracle for me that still makes me shake and brings tears to my eyes when I think about it years later.

Now no one knows to this day what happened to me. Occasionally I have suffered relapses for from one to three months. Back after I exactly had finished the *God Will Never Abandon You!* book and church speaking where God again used me at one church talk so mightily, the night after I had slept all of two hours and He overshadowed me and raised me up to do that talk, (where people told friends of friends in Malta and it got back to me that we saw and heard an amazing church speaker this morning at our church, his name was David Crowder). That encouraged me hugely, as I freely admit that I am not at all a naturally gifted speaker.

I am amazed by God's miracles that He is doing and has already done throughout my life. We don't give up; we know that life is hard. Believe me when I tell you that I personally understand how you may have suffered a lot and continue to suffer with your health even today. God can and will help you if you cry out to Him in your own real desperation and need, with sincere tears from the bottom of your anguished heart, mind, spirit, and soul.

Now you understand why this book is so intensely real and personal for (and to) me. This book is the story of my own life too, told through the stories and prayers of God's heroes like Gideon, King David, King Solomon, King Jehoshaphat, Isaiah, King Hezekiah, and King Josiah. I pray that this encourages you and will lift your spirits.

God will never abandon you in this life! He saved me from the fires of the worst trials that I could possibly bear personally. He saved His heroes in the Bible repeatedly throughout the Old Testament. I cannot encourage you strongly enough to pray these powerful prayers like the ones offered up by King Hezekiah, King David, and King Jehoshaphat, who all cried out to their God for deliverance and saw Him come through every time in a huge, real, and radically life-changing way.

Test God and see if He will not perform such amazing miracles yet again. God still works miracles all over the world today for people of all nationalities, races, and from every kind of backgrounds imaginable. He does them today. He did them yesterday. He will do them again tomorrow! He is that kind of amazing, good, and great God of the universe and of all mankind.

8 THE PRAYER FOR FOGIVENESS FROM KING MANASSEH

Fresh from the excitement, miracles, and power that characterized the reign, life, and prayers of King Hezekiah, you jump back into the time traveling Odyssey. You think back on the lives of the incredible people we have met so far on this amazing journey through the Kingdom of Judah and Ancient Israel. The fearless triumphs of Gideon, the victories and confidence of King David, the glory and wisdom of King Solomon, the desperate deliverance of King Jehoshaphat, the willingness and miracles of Isaiah, and the healing of Hezekiah all dance before your eyes.

The Odyssey stops in front of the son of King Hezekiah. As you climb out and consider the man standing before you and the Kingdom of Judah you see all around, you are stunned. The transformation of the great little God-fearing kingdom is astonishing. What has happened here in only a few decades?

What you see in front of you is not only shocking, but downright emotionally disturbing. The people of Judah are worshipping false gods. They have seemingly abandoned the "faith of their fathers" in only the few years since the death of King Manasseh's glorious father whom God himself called "God's servant" (in the books of the Chronicles of the Kings of Judah, the Second Kings, and the vision of Isaiah).

You don't know how or why this has happened so fast. All that you know is that the people have completely changed in only a single generation. It may have a lot to do with the man standing in front of you.

King Manasseh is the most unlikely of heroes. In fact, at the point in time you see him now, he is no hero, he is a wicked villain. We pick up the story of his great evils against the "God of his fathers" in the book of the Second Chronicles of the Kings of Judah.

> "Manasseh was twelve years old when he became king, and he reigned in Jerusalem fifty-five years. He did evil in the eyes of the Lord, following the detestable practices of the nations the Lord had driven out before the Israelites.
>
> "He rebuilt the high places his father Hezekiah had demolished; he also erected altars to the Baals and made Asherah poles. He bowed down to all the starry hosts and worshipped them. He built altars in the temple of Lord, of which the Lord had said, 'My Name will remain in Jerusalem forever.'
>
> In both courts of the temple of the Lord, he built altars to all the starry hosts. He sacrificed his children in the fire in the Valley of Ben Hinnom, practiced divination and witchcraft, sought omens, and consulted mediums and spiritists. He did much evil in the eyes of the Lord, arousing his anger.
>
> He took the image he had made and put it in God's temple, of which God had said to David and to his son Solomon, 'In this temple and in Jerusalem, which I have chosen out of all

the tribes of Israel, I will put my Name forever. I will not again make the feet of the Israelites leave the land I assigned to your ancestors, if only they will be careful to do everything I have commanded them concerning all the laws, decrees, and regulations given through Moses.'

But Manasseh led Judah and the people of Jerusalem astray, so that they did more evil than the nations the Lord had destroyed before the Israelites." (II Chronicles 33:1-9).

Where do we start in this shocking story? The most horrible thing that King Manasseh (of God's own little country Judah) did in our modern-day eyes was to sacrifice his children in the fire. This should turn your stomach in revulsion. God hates the murder of the innocent, the defenseless, the fatherless, the widows, and the children.

You might be thinking as you read this: "I can't believe any people could be so evil! No wonder God destroyed them in the end, even if they were His little country." Not so fast. Do we not practice and allow abortion, the murder of the innocent and defenseless little children, in nearly every country of the world today? Without wading heavily into this raging debate on abortion here, it is enough to say that what scientists know and doctors admit (however grudgingly) is true--- life begins at conception. It matters intensely to God, and you had better believe that the just and righteous, yet still loving God of the universe and of all mankind is angry at most countries of the world today about it. How can we blame Him for that? You should be angry about it too.

You could argue that God was angry at Manasseh and the people and kingdom of Judah for practicing witchcraft and divination. People do this today again in most nations of the world. Do not think for a moment that this does not matter to God. Why do you think there are so many (and an increasing number of so-called) "acts of God" going on in the world today? Is it only because of global warming?

Or is it the warnings from a just and righteous, loving, but still holy God trying to get our modern day attentions that are so easily diverted by Facebook, Twitter, social media, tablets, smart phones, and the Internet?

You could make the case that God was not pleased with Manasseh and His people the Israelites of the Kingdom of Judah because they set up and worshipped false gods. We would *never* do that! Not unless you consider our modern day false gods that take us away from the real God of all mankind. I could make a whole list of them here. I will in the next chapter on the "Prayer of National Repentance from King Josiah." If you do not know what these false gods are at the moment, I promise that you will soon (next chapter).

Suffice it to say that God had good cause to be angry with the son of the great King Hezekiah and the people of the Kingdom of Jerusalem. Yet in His everlasting mercy, he sent them warnings and messages to try to get their attention the easier way. They opted for the harder way (as we have today).

> "The Lord spoke to Manasseh and his people, but they paid no attention. So the Lord brought against them the army commanders of the king of Assyria, who took Manasseh prisoner, put a hook in his nose, bound him with bronze shackles, and took him to Babylon." (II Chronicles 33:10-11).

I actually go to great lengths describing this horrible punishment of the wicked and evil King Manasseh in my last book *God Will Never Abandon You!* I have also described the torture in horrifying detail in my book from five years ago *The Three Miraculous Prayers of King Hezekiah.* There is no real need to revisit it here and now. All of those things that the verses above said the kings of Assyria did to King Manasseh are mortifying and almost unthinkable in our world today (unless you think back to what ISIS the Islamic State was doing in Iraq, Syria, Egypt, and Libya only a few short years ago).

Reading the terrible evil things that King Manasseh was doing, you cannot help but feel that he deserved the awful torment that he endured as punishment for his many great and evil sins and mistakes against not only the righteous God of the universe, but also against the loving God of all mankind who hated to see innocent children and babies murdered in the fire.

That could have been the end of this story. You might say: "good riddance, the man deserved what he got. Case closed." What makes King Manasseh our unlikely hero in this particular story is shocking and life changing.

Evil King Manasseh Turned to God and Prayed from the Dungeon of the Assyrian Kings

I do not pretend to have all of the answers. Only God knows them all. We do know one thing that this amazing story of King Manasseh tells us is true though. Manasseh did not die in misery as he justly deserved in the dungeons of the Assyrian kings in Babylon.

> "So the Lord brought against them the army commanders of the king of Assyria, who took Manasseh prisoner, put a hook in his nose, bound him with bronze shackles, and took him to Babylon. **In his distress, he sought the favor of the Lord his God and humbled himself greatly before the God of his ancestors. And when he prayed to him, the Lord was moved by his entreaty and listened to his please; so he brought him back to Jerusalem and to his kingdom. Then Manasseh knew that the Lord is God.**" (II Chronicles 33:11-13).

It sends shivers down your spine to read it. What just happened here? King Manasseh hit rock bottom as a result of his mistakes and sins against God and his own children (and even the people of the Kingdom of Judah whom he led astray). Has that ever happened to you before? Maybe you are there right now. Maybe you are reading this needing some hope in your life as a result of the mistakes and choices which you have made. God knows everything and He still forgives us.

Like King Solomon from our earlier chapter famously said, "And when they sin [make mistakes], for all men sin, forgive them..." **(reference from the Chronicles needed, story of the dedication of the temple of King Solomon verse reference goes here please).** He did it for King Manasseh in such a mighty and powerful way then. God specializes in forgiving people like you and me even today. He is the God of all mankind, is anything too hard for Him? He will do it for you personally, right here and now where you are sitting, if only you ask Him to!

Personal Application for Your Life Today

Everyone who knows me understands that I avoid wading into controversy. That is not my style. That said, I do not want to get bogged down in the age-old debate on the Prayer of Manasseh. Let us just say that in countless versions of the Bible throughout well over fifteen years of church history, millions upon millions of people have been saying the prayer of King Manasseh.

It was included in the actual Biblical text of countless versions of the Bible, ranging from the earliest Greek editions of the early church, through the Latin Vulgate, through the translated Bible done by Martin Luther (the father of Protestantism), to the first edition of the King James Bible in the 1600s. It is still found in numerous editions of the Bible in the Anglican Communion and Episcopalian churches and in their Book of Common Prayer, said by millions of Catholics around the world, recited by millions of Orthodox Christians throughout the Balkans, Middle East, and Russia, and used by tens of millions of Protestants throughout dozens of countries around the world.

What I am trying to tell you here is that the Prayer of Manasseh has been included in widely accepted versions of the Bible from all three main branches of the Christian church. One famous church leader mandated that it be reprinted in the preface of an edition of the Bible (centuries ago) so that the Prayer of Manasseh "would not disappear and be lost from the world forever."

Now that we have built up this prayer as it properly deserves, and you understand the impact it has had on not millions of people, not tens of millions of people, but *hundreds of millions of people today and over the last over 1,500 years,* let us take a look at the Prayer of King Manasseh for Forgiveness.

The Prayer that Manasseh Said that So Impressed God

We are looking at the powerful prayer of Manasseh from the Common English Bible Translation. It is also available to you right now in the King James edition of the Bible (and various others) if you are more comfortable with that. We are using this edition as it is in a more easy to understand and current version of English (though I love King James English and its beautiful poetic version of the Bible personally). Read it, and let God change your whole life, just like he did for King Manasseh over 2,500 years ago...

Prayer of Manasseh

Lord Almighty, God of our ancestors,
God of Abraham, Isaac, Jacob,
and their righteous children,
you made heaven and earth
with all their beauty.
You set limits for the sea
by speaking your command.

King Manasseh Cries Out for Forgiveness 1

You closed the bottomless pit,
and sealed it by your powerful
and glorious name.
All things fear you and tremble
in your presence,
because no one can endure
the brightness of your glory.
No one can resist the fury
of your threat against sinners.
But your promised mercies
are beyond measure and imagination,
because you are the highest, Lord,
kind, patient, and merciful,
and you feel sorry over human troubles.

You, Lord, according to
your gentle grace,
promised forgiveness to those
who are sorry for their sins.
In your great mercy,
you allowed sinners to turn
from their sins and find salvation.
Therefore, Lord,
God of those who do what is right,
you didn't offer
Abraham, Isaac, and Jacob,
who didn't sin against you,
a chance to change their hearts and lives.
But you offer me, the sinner,
the chance to change my heart and life,
because my sins outnumbered
the grains of sand by the sea.
My sins are many, Lord; they are many.
I am not worthy to look up,

to gaze into heaven
because of my many sins.

Now, Lord, I suffer justly.
I deserve the troubles I encounter.
Already I'm caught in a trap.
I'm held down by iron chains
so that I can't lift up my head
because of my sins.
There's no relief for me,
because I made you angry,
doing wrong in front of your face,
setting up false gods
and committing offenses.
Now I bow down before you
from deep within my heart,
begging for your kindness.

I have sinned, Lord, I have sinned,
and I know the laws I've broken.
I'm praying, begging you:
Forgive me, Lord, forgive me.
Don't destroy me along with my sins.
Don't keep my bad deeds
in your memory forever.
Don't sentence me to the earth's depths,
for you, Lord, are the God
of those who turn from their sins.

In me you'll show how kind you are.
Although I'm not worthy,
you'll save me according
to your great mercy.

I will praise you continuously
all the days of my life,
because all of heaven's forces praise you,
and the glory is yours
forever and always. Amen.

Wow, what a powerful prayer! I challenge you to find a better prayer of repentance than that one. It changed Manasseh's whole life and future. This prayer moved God's heart in a mighty way that few other prayers have, for a man who was a wicked and evil villain by any reasonable person's measure today. It will change yours today too. Say it and pray it from your heart, like you really mean it!

"Although I am not worthy, you will save me according to your great mercy!"

It makes all the difference in the world. It will open up the floodgates of forgiveness from the living, loving God of the universe and of all mankind.

9 THE PRAYER FROM KING JOSIAH FOR NATIONAL DELIVERANCE

Josiah did not make excuses when a cleansing was needed

As we power up the time traveling Odyssey for one last adventure together in the unforgettable Kingdom of Judah, you find yourself wondering how it will all end in this remarkable tiny kingdom that

God Himself preserved (amid the great powers of the Ancient World) for over 400 years. You ponder why it will have to end when the almighty God of the universe has upheld them through troubles and obstacles that seemed hopelessly impossible for them to overcome on their own.

The answer to this burning question lies in our last stop at the time of the reign of the boy King Josiah. You can see him there as he becomes crowned king at only eight years old! The assassination of his father has caused a profound impact on this young man. He has looked around at the troubles surrounding his new-won kingdom and ponders them for the next eight years until he becomes a man.

By age 16, you see a dramatic choice in the life of this strong, young man standing before you. Josiah makes the remarkable decision at a young and tender age to proactively seek out the God of his fathers. For four years you watch him as he spends time seeking God, learning to know Him personally, and trying to follow His ways.

You can see Josiah now, as he looks around the kingdom four years later and realizes that Judah has become an evil place that has wandered far away from its original purpose as a light to the surrounding nations. This troubles him greatly, and it should. It is clear to Josiah watching his people that they have abandoned God. He wonders in growing disquiet if God will let them go their own way and no longer protect them as He used to. It is clear in the reign of his father that this had already begun to happen to Judah, as the story tells us in the Book of the Kings of Israel and Judah.

> "Josiah was eight years old when he became king, and he reigned thirty-one years in Jerusalem....And he did what was right in the sight of the Lord, and walked in all the ways of his father David; he did not turn aside to the right hand or to the left.
>
> For in the eighth year of his reign, while he was still young, he

began to seek the God of his father David; and in the twelfth year he began to purge Judah and Jerusalem of the high places, the wooden images, the carved images, and the molded images. They broke down the altars of the Bails in his presence, and the incense altars which were above them he cut down; and the wooden images, the carved images, and the molded images he broke in pieces, and made dust of them and scattered it on the grave of those who had sacrificed to them.

He also burned the bones of the priests on their altars, and cleansed Judah and Jerusalem. And so he did in the cities of Manasseh, Ephraim, and Simeon, as far as Naphtali and all around, with axes. When he had broken down the altars and the wooden images, had beaten the carved images into powder, and cut down all the incense altars throughout all the land of Israel, he returned to Jerusalem." (II Kings 22:1-7).

These are the actions of a heroic young king who has turned his heart and mind to serve the living God of the universe not only in the way he talks, but the way he acts. King Josiah took it upon himself to go above and beyond the call of duty too. He was only King of Judah— the Southern Kingdom of the once-united two kingdoms of Israel.

Yet since the Northern Kingdom had already been conquered by the hated Assyrians and the people enslaved and deported in suffering and misery (as told in great and moving detail in my second book *The Three Miraculous Prayers of King Hezekiah*), Josiah took it upon himself to take an entourage comprising priests, officials, and an armed escort of soldiers to ride throughout the borders of the former Northern Kingdom of Israel and to root out the evil there and the worship of false gods there as well.

We can only imagine that the new inhabitants in the north (which the Assyrians had resettled there) were not particularly happy about this turn to the light, but they had no choice in the matter. They were few and scattered throughout the former kingdom of Northern Israel. Josiah exploded onto the scene in the north with Godly might and righteous zeal, unquenchable and unstoppable enthusiasm, and greater physical and military power than they could hope to match. The evil of the false gods was soon completely cleansed and utterly removed.

I know what you're probably thinking right now. All this talk of false gods like Baal, Molech, and Asherah has your head spinning. How does this possibly relate to you today? This is the 21st century; we don't have any false gods anymore, do we?

Not so fast. Our false gods today may not be made out of wood, silver, or gold (and do not resemble monsters from the ancient world), but we absolutely do have them. Today the world offers a slicker and better marketed batch of false gods. If you don't believe me, just get on a bus or walk to a café. Take a look at the people around you; observe them closely for a minute.

I guarantee that you will see many (if not most) of the people on their smart phones and tablets. They are consumed by them as you watch closely. What are they doing? If you look over their shoulders, you will see them surfing through the Internet endlessly, on some kind of silent quest for happiness, purpose, fulfillment, and meaning. Some of them will be texting non-stop, looking for acceptance. Many others will be sighing jealously as they look at pictures of their friends having "wonderful times" and "amazing adventures" on Facebook.

What do these people all have in common? They have most of them become zombies. In a moment of his usual, brilliant insight, Albert Einstein warned many decades ago that this would happen to everybody one day, and he feared it.

He was foreshadowing the latest collection of false gods that people would embrace. We must all guard our own hearts and minds and consider this: what do we spend all of our time talking, thinking about, and doing? It is a good bet whatever that is for you personally, it is your own little false god.

These may not be evil activities in and of themselves. It is the obsession with them (the worship of them) that is the problem. We are all guilty of this here at some point in our lives. We should carefully consider how we spend and use our time that God has given us on this earth.

King Josiah Found A Book of the Law and Prayed

You may be asking yourself as you watch King Josiah cleanse all the land of evil: what caused such a dramatic revival and change of heart in the people of Judah and the king himself? It started a few years earlier with the finding of a book of the law.

> "Hilkiah the high priest said to Shaphan the secretary, 'I have found the Book of the Law in the temple of the Lord.' He gave it to Shaphan, who read it. Then Shaphan the secretary went to the king and reported to him: 'Your officials have paid out the money that was in the temple of the Lord and have entrusted it to the workers and supervisors at the temple.' Then Shaphan the secretary informed the king, 'Hilkiah the priest has given me a book.' And Shaphan read from it in the presence of the king.
>
> When the king heard the words of the Book of the Law, he tore his robes." (II Kings 22:8-11).

Now we come to the heart of the matter with King Josiah. His reaction to hearing the reading of what God wanted from his Kingdom of Judah and the Jewish people was dramatic, real, and immediate. It is a sad testament that God's chosen people had wandered so far away from His will over the previous few kings (especially under King Ammon) that they did not even know what God's law and will were anymore. There are countries like that in the world in which we live today.

Yet it is a great credit to King Josiah that he responded with true repentance in the face of conviction for the evil of his people and his own ignorance of what God wanted from him. He turned his heart to God and to doing what was right. He led the other people around him (his subjects and even people in a rival country the former Kingdom of Northern Israel) in a good and Godly example of doing right as well. This sparked a national revival in short order.

> "He gave these orders to Hilkiah the priest… and Asaiah the king's attendant: 'Go and inquire of the Lord for me and for the people and for all Judah about what is written in this book that has been found. Great is the Lord's anger that burns against us because those who have gone before us have not obeyed the words of this book; they have not acted in accordance with all that is written there concerning us'." (II Kings 22:11-13).

The king's men went to see a prophetess living in Jerusalem to inquire of God what they should do next. The response from God through this prophetess Huldah is eye opening. It has bearing not only for the young man you see standing before you and his repentant and changed people, but also huge relevance for countries of the world today (we will talk all about this in the next chapter).

> "She said to them, 'This is what the Lord, the God of Israel, says: Tell the man who sent you to me, 'This is what the Lord says: I am going to bring disaster on this place and its people, according to everything written in the book the King of Judah has read. Because they have forsaken me and burned incense to other gods and aroused my anger by all the idols their hands have made, my anger will burn against this place and will not be quenched.

> Tell the king of Judah, who sent you to inquire of the Lord,

'This is what the Lord the God of Israel says concerning the words you heard: Because your heart was responsive and you humbled yourself before the Lord when you heard what I have spoken against this place and its people—that they would become a curse and be laid waste—and because you tore your robes and wept in My presence, I also have heard you, declares the Lord. Therefore I will gather you to your fathers, and you will be gathered to your ancestors, and you will be buried in peace. Your eyes will not see all the disaster I am going to bring on this place.' So they took her answer back to the king." (II Kings 22:15-20).

If that passage from the Book of the Kings of Israel and Judah does not give you pause for thought about our own day and age and what is going on in the world today, then nothing will.

If you take a look around the world at all of the disasters you see going on now, you might simply write them off as "global warming." Or you might look deeper, with eyes that see and ears that hear. You might stop and realize that most nations of the world today have abandoned the "God of their fathers" even as Judah did over 2,500 years ago. The results in our world today are much like they were in the days of the last kings of Judah. It is a sad case study of what can happen when people turn away from God. More importantly though it is a warning and a wakeup call to us all living in the world today.

Personal Application for Your Life Today

Josiah passionately prayed a prayer. We do not know the precise words; they were not recorded. It must be in this particular case that the exact words which Josiah said were not what moved God's heart to mercy. We do know all about the king's *attitude and actions* in this prayer though. The prophetess told us everything.

81

God said that He had seen Josiah's actions. There are three actual things (according to the words of the prophetess Huldah in the passage above) the king did that impressed God so much that he put off the natural punishments for nations turning against Him:

1. Josiah *humbled himself* and showed a responsive heart to the *evil that his people had been doing for years*. This mattered hugely to the almighty God, and it still does today.

2. The king tore his robes to show his *sincerity of repentance*. You see the man standing before you. This is not cheap clothing he is tearing up. He is a king wearing costly garments. Josiah demonstrated his earnest physical and spiritual level of anguish over their collective national sins this way. You do not have to tear up the clothing you are wearing right now to show God that you are sorry. There are many ways of sincerely expressing your sorrow (for your own mistakes and those of your nation) to God. Remember that while "man looks on the outward appearance, God looks on the heart." (I Samuel 16:7)

3. Josiah wept before God. God said, "I have seen your tears in My presence." This is now the second time we witnessed a prayer that moved the heart of God which was accompanied by tears (like King Hezekiah before Josiah). King David also wept before God when he repented (see Psalms).

These "men after God's own heart" are trying to tell us all something here today. When you are truly sorry for your mistakes and the things that we have all done wrong, then real sorrow and repentance are accompanied by tears. This may not be a popular idea in our tough guy culture today, but it reflects the condition and confession of your heart still. If you want to move God with your prayers today, take heed of this example. Make sure that the tears are sincere (and not crocodile tears).

When was the last time you have made such an earnest and heartfelt demonstration before God in your own personal and private prayer time? No one else is there to see you but God Himself, after all. What is stopping you from really sharing your heart through prayers that are about more than just the usual (same old) words? It is all about a radical change of lifestyle and a shift of attitude in prayer. Anyone can do it if you are only willing.

God has promised us a second chance as nations today in His word that does not change and endures forever. "If my people, who are called by my name, will humble themselves and pray and seek my face and turn from their wicked ways, then I will hear from heaven, and I will forgive their sin and will heal their land." (II Chronicles 7:14). This promise from the Lord God of the universe and the God of all mankind can give you real hope and a driving divine purpose in your own daily life, even today.

One man (or woman) can make a difference. This is your time to be the change for your own nation. Follow the prayer and example of King Josiah and watch and see what God will do in your own life and for your country. It often takes many people in a nation to change the course of their collective destiny in God's eyes. The great news is that it all starts with one person like you today (right here and now) saying one powerful prayer just like good King Josiah did 2,500 years ago.

10 WHAT IT ALL MEANS FOR YOUR COUNTRY TODAY

We have come far together in the brief pages of this book, through hundreds of years of time traveling odyssey. The stories that you have seen and the prayers that you have heard across the land of Israel and throughout the kingdom of Judah are just as relevant and powerful today as they were nearly three thousand years ago. A great example of this and how it impacts you today has to do with the nation in which you live now in our own modern times of the twenty-first century.

The Bible tells us that God governs the affairs of men and nations (Isaiah 66). This was true in the time of the ancient Israelites and the Kingdom of Judah. It is still true in our own world today. You do not have to take my word for it. You can look all around you and see the principles of righteousness and prayers all at work in the countries of the world still.

The nations that have abandoned God suffer for it. It is not that He necessarily causes the suffering (He allows people and nations to walk away from Him and His divine protection when they wish). These are the principles from these historical stories recorded in the Old Testament of the Bible still at work in our world even today.

A Real-World, Modern Day Example of These Truths and Prayers At Work

You can look at a nation like Haiti for an example of a place that chose to abandon God completely. The history of their rebellion against Him dates back to the slave revolt of Toussaint Louverture. It took the slaves a mere twenty years to turn what was once one of the most prosperous places in the world (sugar cane production made it fantastically wealthy) into one of the most, if not the most, impoverished lands in the history of mankind.

God did not cause the misery and suffering that has resulted. The slaves who revolted against the knowledge of Him and who drove out the Europeans did this all by themselves. They created a new religion called voodoo based on elements of African tribal religions and witchcraft that is very much against God. They went on a deliberate rampage throughout the island, burning and destroying all signs of wealth and forms of production so that no one would want to take over their land again. It was a real-world scorched earth policy that left the island in terrible shape.

It is an interesting contrast though that the island was two nations, living side by side (much like the Kingdoms of Northern Israel and Judah in fact).

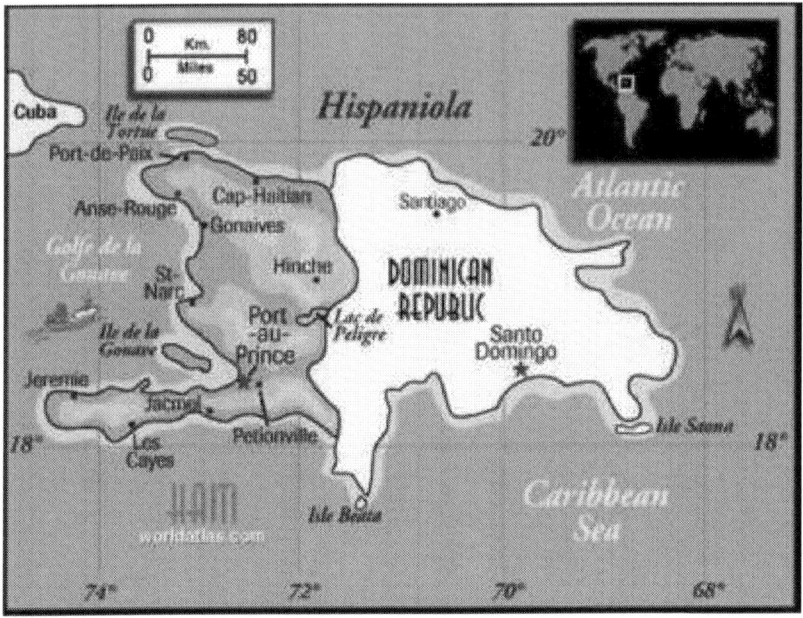

The Eastern two-thirds of the island held on to their traditional Christianity in the Dominican Republic. They refused to abandon God and turn against the knowledge of Him. They fought back against the marauding and murdering slaves who had driven the French out of Haiti and were determined to do the same to the Dominican Republic (run by the Spanish at the time). Did God help the people in the DR who held on to Him then?

Against all odds in the face of the terror and reckless hate that was the Haitian slave revolt, the Christian people of the DR prevailed and drove the slaves back to the original boundaries between French Haiti and the Spanish Dominican Republic lands. The advance and destruction of the terror was stopped and quelled.

Interestingly enough, the two countries diverged from this point forward. Haiti stubbornly clung to its anti-God religion which the slaves had created with their witchcraft (something the Bible condemns in the strongest possible terms – see the story of King Saul of Israel and the Witch of Endor, I Samuel 28), much as the northern Kingdom of Israel in our story earlier continued to worship false gods and practice the murder of babies in sacrifice to the abhorrent gods Molech and Baal.

Meanwhile the Dominican Republic embraced its culture of Christianity. They did not burn and close down their churches or drive out the priests and pastors. They held on to their knowledge of the God of all mankind ("I am the LORD, the God of all mankind. Is anything too hard for me?" Jeremiah 32:27) staunchly and refused to let go. In a sense, they were like (an imperfect mirror of) the Kingdom of Judah. The DR was and is still today a God-fearing land.

While Haiti's situation went from bad to worse economically over the following centuries, the Dominican Republic's continued to be stable and improve. In time the Spanish granted the people of the DR their independence. Industries continued to thrive (mostly sugar cane, the DR is still one of the world's largest producers of it). Tourism boomed in the Dominican Republic. Economic and social development proceeded gradually and mostly steadily. The country today is not wealthy, but it is infinitely better off than its immediate neighbor. Crucially, they still hold on to the "God of their fathers." How devoted they are or not is for God to judge. Yet the proverbial proof is in the pudding when you compare them to their neighboring country Haiti.

There is also something else interesting at work behind the scenes in the Dominican Republic. During the run up to and the time following the Second World War, President Trujillo the Dominican Republic leader welcomed in God's people the Jews (who were the people of the Kingdoms of Northern Israel and Judah) to allow them to immigrate to the Dominican Republic.

He gave them a safe haven (Liechtenstein also did this in the Second World War, and look at the tiny principality today--- it is among the wealthiest on earth). The Bible tells us that God will "bless those who bless you and curse him who curses you…" (Genesis 12:3). In fact you could make the case from this verse that a nation's successes or failures throughout human history have been a reflection of this Biblical truth regarding how they treated the Israelites/Jews, who were and still are God's chosen people.

Without getting into the political or cultural reasons for why the DR President Trujillo did what he did, He still blessed the Jewish people by providing them a refuge in their greatest time of suffering as a people. God took notice too, as He promised to in that verse above. The Dominican Republic has prospered hugely for this in the intervening years.

As an example, one of the world's largest sausage makers today is based in the Dominican Republic. This provides a great national export and a boost to the local economy. The people who founded this business were some of the Jewish refugees whom Trujillo welcomed into the country. He helped to save them from a likely death at the hands of the anti-God Nazis of Second World War Germany. God's promises are just as real today as they were thousands of years ago my friends.

Haiti on the other hand deforested their part of the island of Hispaniola over the years. With no trees left to speak of, the rich soil that the entire island had been famous for simply eroded and washed away in heavy tropical rains and storms (never to be recovered once it is gone) across Haiti (but not in the neighboring DR). This caused natural disasters in Haiti to become worse than imaginable since there were no trees left to break strong winds from occasional hurricanes, nor to hold the earth together when flash floods happened, nor to stop the resulting landslides (that have devastating effects sometimes there).

You could make the claim that Haiti is under a terrible judgment or even a curse looking at it today. A number of people call it the poorest country on earth. Without a doubt it holds a spot in the top several poorest nations according to economists and the United Nations. Remember that only two hundred plus years ago, Haiti was among the richest lands in the world. It is so like the contrasting stories of the Kingdom of Northern Israel and the Kingdom of Judah.

You can do the math yourself as to what happened in these two countries. People made choices, they abandoned God (or held on to him), and He let them go on their vastly different ways. The difference between these two neighboring countries today is striking and even breathtaking. They were virtually identical only a few centuries ago (apart from Spanish and French speaking languages). The principles of the Bible are just as true today as they were 2,500 to 3,000 years ago.

You can also say that God judges the nations (Isaiah 66) for their various actions and choices that are either for or against Him. Haiti not only turned its collective national back on him (like the Northern Kingdom of Israel did), but they embraced anti-God false religions and witchcraft in their practice of voodoo (again like Northern Israel). They have suffered from devastating earthquakes, hurricanes, floods and more over the intervening centuries and especially in the last twenty to thirty years.

The damage has been tragic, devastating, and lasting. People there today suffer horribly. It brings tears to your eyes to watch the news footage of their plight. Yet still they have not returned to the living God of all mankind that their ancestors once knew and respected.

Meanwhile in the Dominican Republic neighboring state, most of the population remains staunchly Christian and God-fearing. They go to church. They do not allow or practice abortion, which is still the murder of the innocent and unborn in the eyes of the Lord God.

It matters to God, my friends. It always has and it always will. Whatever their shortcomings or imperfections are, God sees the DR's national stance regarding Him. Next we'll consider a place that is as close to my heart as it is to God's, the Mediterranean island nation that we have called home for the last three years and where my son Alex was born before that six and a half years ago.

Example of Malta that Held on to Its Knowledge of and Respect for God

Now we turn our attention to another modern day example of what can happen when a nation refuses to let go of their knowledge of and faith in God. This is the three island nation of the Republic of Malta (and Gozo). In 2010, we had the privilege of coming here for the first time. We only stayed for three months on that trip, but we quickly discovered something interesting and almost unique about Malta that has never ceased to amaze me over the years that we have been back and lived here.

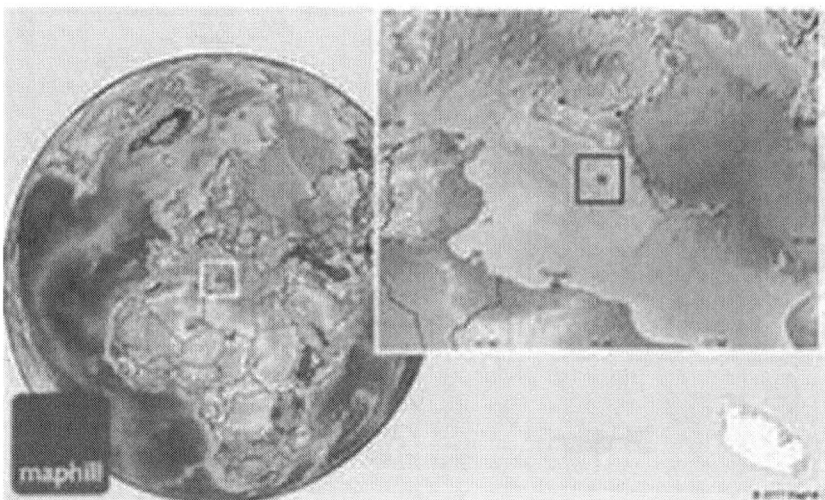

2Map Showing Location of Malta

I first noticed it when going to government offices, hospitals (with my health problems I have suffered from in the past), and doctor's offices (polyclinics). When you walk in the door, one of the first things that strikes your eyes (especially if you are paying attention to your surroundings) is a cross hanging on the wall. My very first time to walk into a government office here in Malta, I saw posters with bible verses and nature scenes plastered on office doors of government officials.

Years after first living here, I encountered an exciting group called the EU of Prayer (that follows the rotating EU presidency around Europe every six months to meet with government leaders and understand the nation so that they can pray for it). At this meeting, they told us that when they went into Malta's Parliament to observe a session of government, the parliament opened with everyone in the chamber saying "The Lord's Prayer" (Matthew 6:9-13). The British man who heads up the group said that he was astounded by not only this powerful prayer that the parliamentarians said, but the fact that a large cross with Jesus hanging on it was looking down over the parliamentarians as they hold session. With great emotion he told us that they had *never seen this anywhere else* in the entire 28 nation member European Union.

We quickly learned living here that abortion is illegal (it is now the only nation left in Europe to my knowledge where that is the case since Ireland abandoned their God-fearing position on this issue that is so very important to God). At the time, even divorce was illegal (today is it allowed in somewhat limited cases with waiting, cooling off periods). The people and government of Malta staunchly defend their cultural and historic Christian faith that they have practiced since the time that Paul and Luke shipwrecked in Malta over 1,960 years ago (as told in Acts of the Apostles chapter 28), bringing the light of Christianity and fuller knowledge of God to the island.

The Maltese have a huge festival each year in Valletta that commemorates this special event. They celebrate it with an enormous street party outside of the Church of St. Paul's Shipwreck in the capital with fireworks, bands, and more. What struck me most about it is their enormous banners that read Paul, Father of the Maltese. Paul was the greatest missionary of the early church and a person God used to spread the good news of Jesus Christ throughout the

Roman Mediterranean world.

Like any nation in the world, the country of Malta is not perfect, the people are not all saints, the government ministers have their issues, and certainly not everyone faithfully attends church here as they did in the past. It is for God to judge the hearts of these individual people and where they are at with Him. But we can draw lessons from the state of this blessed nation based on their national reverence for God and His representatives from the early church (Paul and Luke).

Do not think that this does not matter to God. Consider for a few moments how Malta is doing today as a country. They have been unnaturally (supernaturally) blessed when so many of the far larger and more populous and powerful nations in Europe have suffered from terrible problems over the last few decades (some have nearly failed as going concerns).

Malta has no natural resources of any kind whatsoever, except for the usually dependable hot sun, the surrounding Mediterranean Sea, and an enormous treasure trove of historical sites--- 365 historic churches (that were literally built with the intention of having one for every day of the year), three walled cities, and numerous towers and forts scattered widely around the two main islands of Malta and Gozo. As friends of mine in Eastern Europe have told me in the past though, you can't eat historical attractions.

The country was desperately poor when the British withdrew more than forty years ago. Yet in the intervening years, the country has absolutely blossomed into one of the greatest success stories the world has seen economically in the post-World War II era. The economy is far stronger than it should be for a country of only less than half a million people that is 125 square miles in total size. This makes only the Ocala National Forest next to Ocala where we lived years ago in Florida larger than the entire nation of Malta.

The government budgets are balanced and even have surpluses. Malta's government has spare cash reserves to spend on things like free healthcare and childcare for everyone. Speaking of healthcare, they have been named the fourth best healthcare system in the world by the World Health Organization.

That was before the country built and paid for (all by itself) what was the largest hospital in all of Europe (Mater Dei) when it was built a few years ago, and where my son was born just over six years ago. When you walk in it looks like an airport terminal. It has over 9,000 hospital beds in a facility that boasts as many as seven floors and is comprised of multiple enormous buildings that some would call a small town. I have been lost in those corridors before, but thankfully the people of Malta are kind and free with directions even in their biggest, world-class hospital.

You rarely see a homeless person in the country. I have been stopped and asked to help the poor in Malta on a handful of occasions in more than four years spent living here. Everyone who wants a job has one. People come to Malta from Italy, Spain, and Greece to find work all the time. I have met some of them personally asking me where they could go to find a job, right off of the ferry boats.

The unemployment rate here is half that of "rich and powerful" countries like France and Germany. Spain and Greece have four to five times as high an unemployment rate as Malta does today. When Malta offered a ground breaking program in Europe to sell its citizenship and EU-approved passports to wealthy individuals, the program was double oversubscribed. This netted the government of Malta an enormous windfall amounting to hundreds of millions of euros (a fortune in a nation with less than half a million people).

The real estate market is booming like no other place in the European Union's (soon to be) 27 countries. Construction companies have far more work than they can handle and have told friends of mine that they turn away jobs. Even in the small seaside town in which we live here (with a population of under 15,000 people) there are approximately 10 cranes building at a time right now.

The waters around Malta are statistically the cleanest in Europe. The pollution level is among the lowest in Europe. Crime is the lowest in the 28 countries of the EU by far. Violent crime is extremely rare and huge national news when it happens. There has never been a single school shooting or known mass shooting incident in Malta.

Tourism in Malta amounts to between five and six million visitors a year from the flights that keep the airport humming around the clock and the modern cruise port that welcomes sometimes three cruise ships in a single day. This amounts to between 12 and 15 tourists per person per year. It would be like Great Britain welcoming over 750 million tourists a year, or the United States hosting nearly four billion tourists annually. A significant cruise line MSC moved its headquarters to Malta. Countless trading ships have registered in Malta, providing a significant income for the country whose stability in a troubled and dark world has become something of a legend. The Malta Free Trade Port at Birzebbuga is busy year round. The country has a booming industry in repairing and resupplying passing ships that traverse the Mediterranean. It has diversified into pharmaceutical production, beverage manufacturing, offshore banking and insurance, offshore gambling, and even now has just become the new home country host of the world's largest crypto currency exchange that used to be based in Japan.

Malta is consistently rated as among the top ten best places in the world to retire and live (International Living Magazine) for its low crime, quality of life, cost of living relative to larger European destinations, pace of life, stability, and constant activity. The country has been rated one of the happiest nations on earth. The Maltese people show it in their generally kind and welcoming, helpful nature. I regularly hear people walking around singing or whistling in the streets. This is a rare occurrence in many other larger, more powerful, more "successful" nations on earth today. It is the many blessings of God my friends.

Yet, the country is not perfect. It has begun to slowly turn away from God over the last several years. I have noticed the difference even in the eight years since we first came to the islands. And with a departure from God, as we saw throughout this story in the Kingdom of Judah (and in my previous book _The Three Miraculous Prayers of King Hezekiah_), problems have slowly but persistently begun to appear here.

There are now more frequent social problems than there were even a decade ago. Many people have stopped attending church and ceased to be devout in their reverence to God, deciding to go it alone. This is what happens to countries many times when they become incredibly prosperous. As with the Kingdom of Judah throughout its history that we saw in our time traveling odyssey, the Maltese people gradually begin to attribute their success and relative prosperity to their own efforts, smart business practices, and wise governance. Sadly, the abundant blessings of God slowly begin to be withdrawn.

The younger generations are particularly troubled (and not coincidentally the least interested in going to church). Many of them do not know God so personally or with such devotion as their parents and grandparents have (so like the Kingdom of Judah). Depression and drug use are increasing. Unwed pregnancies have been steadily rising. Gay marriage was passed in parliament, divorce was made legal, marriage is becoming increasingly less common, divorce rates are climbing.

Yet as all nations inevitably go their own way and depart from their devotion to God with time, there is still hope for a return to the "faith of their fathers." Many people here still fight the good fight to halt the advance of evil and poor national and personal choices. This also matters hugely to God.

For example, the bulwark of people, churches, and the government fighting to keep abortion illegal here is still solid. This is one of the critical remaining moral pillars in Malta that matters enormously to God for nations. Consider how much God hated the sacrificing of newborn babies, infants, and children on the horrific altars to Baal and Molech in the stories we have witnessed together earlier in the book.

Besides this, the cross is still everywhere in Malta, and this matters to God too. You see Jesus saves you, Jesus loves you, and Jesus heals you signs all over Malta. Whether or not the majority of the people believes this or not is not the point here. A significant minority still does and they proclaim it constantly through crosses, pictures of Jesus, Bible verse nature posters, and the sticker messages. More and more churches are springing up everywhere across the island. This matters hugely to God.

What it means is that Malta is a mixed bag in God's eyes, like every nation under the sun today. Yet they can still boast being more God-fearing in critical areas that matter to God. As one young Maltese man I buy chicken and mushroom pies from told me when he heard about my Christian books, "right on man, we're very faithful to God here." It tips the proverbial scales in His eyes in their favor, even though He sees and does not like the rising problems, poor national choices, and the gradually encroaching spread of evil. It is a warning for Malta and many other nations of the world.

But What Can I Do About It?

It is a sobering reminder to us all that *there is something we can do about it.* You can pray without ceasing for the country in which you live. Maybe your own country has abandoned God or does not even know Him at all. This does not stop you from praying for your nation and people, your national leaders and politicians.

Pray that they will make the right choices that please God. The Bible tells us that God appoints the rulers of nations ("He changes times and seasons; he deposes kings and raises up others. He gives wisdom to the wise and knowledge to the discerning. "Daniel 2:21) and to "submit to the governing authorities." ("Everyone must submit himself to the governing authorities, for there is no authority except that which is from God. The authorities that exist have been appointed by God." Romans 13:1). Live your own life as a shining example of Godliness and in obedience to His commands that He shared with us in the Bible.

Be an ambassador of the light of God to your own country and for your nation to the rest of a dark, lost, and terribly hurting world. The former President of Malta once said it so beautifully and movingly in a welcoming speech that he gave before European Union representatives. He said that Europe needs Malta because Malta is a light shining in the darkness of Europe. I have never forgotten this touching national speech from only a few years ago. You can be sure that God remembers it as well.

There is so very much that you can do personally in the land that you call home. Take heart and do not be discouraged, but rise up and fight the good, Godly fight for the truth and His light. Pray without ceasing. Share God's love with everyone you encounter on a daily basis whenever you can.

You may not think that you are personally up to the challenge at hand. You may say that "I am not King David, King Solomon, King Hezekiah, King Jehoshaphat, King Josiah, Gideon, or Isaiah" whose lives we witnessed on our unforgettable time-traveling adventure throughout this story of encouragement, miracles, answers to prayer, and hope. Remember that the great news is this: Fortunately God specializes in working with imperfect people like you and me; we are all that He has to work with after all.

11 WHAT IT MEANS FOR YOU PERSONALLY

If ever there was a time that we needed a mighty deliverance in all of our lives, it is now! Consider the whole world around you today. It is a complete and total mess. Looking at the world now, you see natural disasters everywhere. Flash fires killing nearly a hundred people in their pain and anguish in Greece outside of Athens; wild fires sweeping across California and destroying homes and people's very lives so fast that they have no chance to even run from them; and people starving to death without hope, without help, without anyone to save them from their pain and sorrow in Eastern Europe, Africa, and Asia all remind you that the world today needs God desperately. Let's be completely real and honest here a minute and say that *you* need God desperately and personally. *We all do.*

People need hope; people need answers. They need a personal touch from the Lord God Almighty of the universe, from the God of all mankind, from the God of peace, from the God of healing, from the God of love, from the God who is your provider, from the God who promised that He will never leave you or forsake you and that He is with you always to the very end of the world, from the God who loves you so very much that you cannot even imagine it!

I would never pretend to have all of the answers. Like you, like all of us, I am also a man on an individual and daily spiritual quest to know

God on a more personal and real level in my own everyday life. Yet these prayers are the words given to us by the Lord God Himself through the stories faithfully recorded in the Bible over 2,500 years ago. They are not my own stories; they are the stories that God gave us to be shining examples and to offer real hope and encouragement to us all. They are the truth of the stories that we have been privileged to witness together on our time-traveling Odyssey through the triumph and tragedy, miracles, hope, and especially the most powerful prayers from the Kingdom of Judah.

We learn so very much from these true stories and the powerful prayers. As a conclusion, we will look at a summary of the lessons that you have seen throughout the course of this book here before doing a recap of the 7 Most Powerful Prayers from the Kingdom of Judah. They are the words that God gave us to change our lives and the lives of those suffering and hurting all around us every day in a lost and dying world. They matter for today; they matter forever.

Summary of What We Have Learned on This Odyssey for Our Own Lives

1. **Gideon God's Mighty Warrior -** *"Lord Show Me A Sign That You Are With Me Today, Please take away my fear and make me like Gideon the Strong and not Gideon the Weak."* – he needed four major miraculous signs from God in order to have the courage to overcome his fears and to do what God asked of him (to be the man he was meant to be). Do not be afraid to ask God for signs that He will be with you and will help you in your own life.

2. **King David the original "Man After God's Own Heart" -** *"Those Who Know Your Name Trust in You, For You O Lord Never Forsake Those Who Seek You."* & *"I have not seen the righteous forsaken nor the children of the righteous begging for bread."* - King David trusted God

completely and saw huge miracles throughout his whole life, for his hopeless financial condition, and even for his daily survival. We can all aspire to be like the great man in his many finest hours, and try to avoid his mistakes in his worst moments. He is a mighty man (called by some the world's first "Renaissance Man") to whom we can all relate in some way. Let us set ourselves to be King David the heroic (and not King David the moral disappointment).

3. **King Solomon the Wisest Mortal Man Who Ever Lived –** *"Give me wisdom and a discerning heart"* - Make your prayers ones that please God. King Solomon trusted God would give him great wisdom and discernment to govern the great two nations that he had inherited from his father David (Kingdoms of Judah and Israel). His prayer for wisdom so impressed God that He made a one of a kind offer to the man whom He loved like a son.

God gave Solomon something unique in all of human history! He became the wisest man who ever lived and the wealthiest in his day, and one of the richest, most honored, most famous people in all of recorded history. Yet he was not without his faults either, as he let the distraction and allure of many godless women turn his heart cooler to God in the second half of his life. Solomon is a fantastic example and a serious warning to us all about what can happen when we pray big prayers and also what can happen to us when we take our eyes and focus off of God and let ourselves be distracted by the many "enticing things" all around us.

Remember that God did not promise to make you rich. He could do it tomorrow if He wanted to, but the truth is that He would rather you be humble and dependent on Him than to have your eyes taken off of Him and turned to the false god of materialism. He is pleased to make you rich in spirit though, and that is a far greater "treasure" than any wealth that this frail and passing world could ever offer you! He will gladly do this for you if only you sincerely ask Him to (just like Solomon himself did).

4. **King Jehoshaphat the Overcomer –** *"We do not know what to do, but our eyes are on you!"* - If ever there was a time when we needed powerful and life- changing deliverance in our lives, it is now! There is no better story of God's miraculous deliverance (that I have ever seen) than the ones of King Jehoshaphat and King Hezekiah (I wrote all about Hezekiah's other miraculous deliverances in my prior book *The Three Miraculous Prayers of King Hezekiah: A Good Man's Example for Our Own Troubled Times*. This is the real power and miracles of God in action. These miraculous prayers still work today, if only you ask God to save you in your distress!

5. **Isaiah, Judah's Greatest Prophet –** *"I am here, I am willing, I will go. Lord send me!"* - If we were all willing to go and serve God and others like Isaiah the prophet did, the world would be a far happier, more peaceful, better place. The media once asked a great and successful pastor of a large mega church in America, "When are you most like Jesus, pastor?" His answer stayed with me all these years. The pastor said, "When I am setting up the chairs before the church service, I am most like Jesus."

Let's all try to be like that. You will find no better, greater adventure and calling in your life. This provides all of the purpose and meaning that you could ever hope for in an otherwise mostly meaningless world. It satisfies so much more than money, fame, power, or pleasure ever can.

6. **King Hezekiah "God's Servant" –** *"I have walked faithfully before you my whole life,"* *a prayer from a*

broken heart accompanied by tears – Maybe you have walked faithfully and loyally before God your whole life. If so, this prayer is even more powerful and especially relevant to you.

When we are in dire need though (whatever our life has been like) and we cry out to God, He is watching and listening closely. The prayers that move the heart of God are the ones where he sees our desperate need, expressed from the depths of our anguished heart, mind, and soul.

7. **King Manasseh the Evil Ruler Turned Forgiven Hero –** *"Although I am not worthy, you will save me according to your great mercy!"* Manasseh is the easiest for us to relate to when we have made a mess of our lives. No one could outdo Manasseh for the evil that he did (at the time). There are consequences for terrible mistakes that we make or evil that we do, as the life of Manasseh showed us in such sobering detail.

Yet his story to me has always been one of hope. No matter how much we have done wrong in our days on earth, or how many ways that we have disappointed God with our choices, we can still find forgiveness from God and restoration in our lives.

8. **King Josiah the National Revival Leader** – We do not have the words from King Josiah's prayer, only the way that he prayed. It makes this one a "bonus" beyond the seven most powerful prayers, but it is so relevant and important for our lives and the nations which we call home. Pray with sincere and real tears to show God that you are desperate for forgiveness in your own life and for your own nation.

In my own life, I have wept before God for my sins, for my many personal needs, for the needs of others hurting all around me, and for the land in which I live. God has done great and mighty things on my behalf repeatedly. It is not because of who I am, but because of who *He* is, and because of these prayer examples and accompanying promises in His word! It will work for you too today, my friends!

It is no accident that we are still talking about all of these stories and prayers 3,000 to 2,500 years after they happened… and we are still talking about them. Say these prayers again and again in and over your own life. It will fundamentally change the way in which you live your days that God has given you upon this earth. This is what matters after all.

7 Most Powerful Prayers For Your Own Life

1. "Lord Show Me A Sign That You Are With Me Today; Please take away my fear and make me like Gideon the Strong and not Gideon the Weak!" (He will do it!)

2. "Those Who Know Your Name Trust in You, For You O Lord Never Forsake Those Who Seek You." "I have not seen the righteous forsaken nor the children of the righteous begging for bread!" (He will not abandon you!)

3. "God give me wisdom and a discerning heart!" (He gives wisdom generously!)

4. "We do not know what to do, but our eyes are on you!" (He will save you!)

5. "I am here, I am willing, I will go. Lord send me!" (He will honor that!)

6. "I have walked faithfully before you my whole life" **a prayer from a broken heart accompanied by tears.** (He will heal you!)

7. "Although I am not worthy, you will save me according to your great mercy!" (He will forgive you right here, right now!)

12 AND THEN IT'S ALL OVER IN THE BLINK OF AN EYE

As I sit writing this story of hope, encouragement, and miracles, my eyes were drawn to the top headline story on the Yahoo! News homepage. Tragically it reads, "They're all gone in the blink of an eye." The headline story reminds us all of our own frailty and ultimate mortality…

A family of six individuals hailing from New Jersey was returning from a trip when their vehicle was hit hard by a pickup truck that swerved across the median and finally careened into the opposite lane. The ensuing crash killed the New Jersey father and all four of his daughters with him. The lone survivor was the devastated mother who survived the crash and is now left behind. She probably wishes that she had died with the rest of her family. The mother's life has been horribly changed forever.

This tragic true story should give us all pause for thought about the real meaning of our relatively short lives. The Bible tells us that we are no more than a vapor.

> "Why, you do not even know what will happen tomorrow. What is your life? You are a mist that appears for a little while and then vanishes." (James 4:14).

This is to say that you are here today and gone tomorrow. We're all literally going, going, gone.

None of us can say with any certainty whatsoever when we will draw our final breath. It means that life is short, and we should make each and every day count. This starts by praying hard, without ceasing whenever you can in your own daily circumstances. It is a radical change of lifestyle that will make all the difference for your purpose and meaning in your days here on this earth. It all starts with a small but powerful prayer (like the ones you saw from the Kingdom of Judah throughout this book).

The next takeaway from this story above is to live your life every day as best you possibly can to the full potential that God intended for you personally. Finally, you need to realize the truth that one day—today, tomorrow, next week, next month, next year, ten years from now, or in the future at some point for certain—you will stand before the great and mighty God of the universe to give an accounting for how you spent your days on this earth.

If that sounds terrifying to you right now, it does not have to be. You can face that eventual and inevitable day of divine personal reckoning with confidence, hope, and peace. All that you have to do is say this powerful prayer below fervently, from your heart, and you will be ready to meet your maker God (who loves you so very much) when your time comes at last…

A Prayer to Reconcile You to God

Pray this simple but powerful prayer and God almighty will save you: Father God, I thank you for sending your son Christ Jesus to die on the cross for me and my sins. I believe that He rose again from the dead and is now seated at Your right hand. Father God, from the bottom of my heart I want to repent and ask for forgiveness for all of my sins (things I have done wrong). Please forgive me. I want to trust Jesus alone as my Lord and Savior. Please come into my heart and dwell in me. I believe salvation cannot be bought or earned. I want to accept this free gift of salvation. Fill me with your Holy Spirit. Thank you for forgiveness and Your gift of everlasting life that I have in Christ Jesus.

That was it! Now you can grow in your new faith in Christ Jesus by reading your Bible every day (start with the book of John/Gospel According to John), by praying to your Heavenly Father God as a child speaks to his dad, and by regularly attending a Bible preaching church.

ABOUT THE AUTHOR

W.D. Crowder is a five-time American published Christian author, financial journalist, prolific article writer, and international speaker. He has penned over 3,500 commissioned articles and written/designed hundreds of financial web pages and newsletter posts.

Crowder researched and wrote his latest book in the island nation of Malta in the Mediterranean Sea, where he lives with his wife and two children. W.D. Crowder has spoken at a variety of church services and Christian group meetings in the United States and Europe and done interviews for a number of radio station programs in the United States and Great Britain.

A widely read and top of his class graduate of Stetson University, he obtained his bachelor of arts degree in History with minors in Latin American Studies and International Relations and a special emphasis in Economics. He was President of his Phi Alpha Theta (National History Honors Fraternity) Stetson University chapter and a Phi Beta Kappa member.

W. D. Crowder has published five books in his exciting Divine Encounters of the Bible Series, including 7 Most Powerful Prayers from the Kingdom of Judah: Fearlessness, Hope, and Miracles for Your Everyday Circumstances, We Three Kings: Two Journeys of the Magi, The Three Miraculous Prayers of King Hezekiah: A Good Man's Example for Our Own Troubled Times, Lives of the Great Apostles: The Real Life Rest of the Story of the Men Who Walked Beside Jesus, and God Will Never Abandon You! Biblical and Personal Examples of God's Everlasting Faithfulness.

Printed in Poland
by Amazon Fulfillment
Poland Sp. z o.o., Wrocław